Cebu

Cebu

PETER BACHO

UNIVERSITY OF WASHINGTON PRESS

Seattle and London

Copyright © 1991 by the University of Washington Press
Third printing (pbk.), 1999
Printed in the United States of America

Library of Congress Cataloging-in-Publication Data
Bacho, Peter.
Cebu / Peter Bacho.
p.   cm.
ISBN 0-295-97132-0 (alk. paper)
I. Title.
PS3552.A2573C4 1991   91-323
813'.54—dc20   CIP

The paper used in this publication is acid-free and recycled from 10 percent
post-consumer and at least 50 percent pre-consumer waste. It meets the
minimum requirements of American National Standard for Information
Sciences—Permanence of Paper for Printed Library Materials,
ANSI Z39.48-1984. ♾ ♽

Contents

Cebu

Prologue:
Going Home

As the jetliner flew toward Cebu, it rattled like an old Ford on the freeway. Years ago it was deemed unsafe for U.S. skies, but like so much of America's obsolescence, it found a new home in the Philippines.

Passengers in the plane's half-filled cabin were as silent as eggs in a carton, and almost as white. Twenty minutes out of Manila, less than an hour from Cebu, a storm had hit, turning the skies black. The first big shake opened the luggage bins overhead and sent tumbling any people unlucky enough to be standing.

Now Cebu was just ahead, and all experienced travelers noted with marked gratitude the plane's slight descent and reduction in speed, items on a checklist required to land. First-time fliers had no such relief. One who didn't was Ben Lucero, a priest from the States with a lot on his mind. He was taking the body of his mother, Remedios, home to Cebu for burial. This was really his second flight, the first being yesterday's flight from Seattle to Manila. With each jolt, Ben squeezed the ends of his arm rests until he thought he felt the metal bend.

"Whew," he whispered after the last bad bump. Ben knew that fear had frozen most of him, the promise of eternal life notwithstanding. Here and now he had a promise to keep, son to mother, and it was all he could do to summon up faith in the pilot. Prayers to God seemed suddenly wide of the mark—a direct line to the cockpit would be more on target. He resolved to make a noise, however humble. What he wanted most to do was scream something primal and profane—"Jesus Christ almighty, man, let's get this crate to Cebu!"—but he decided against it. Stressed as he was, he knew he couldn't handle the syllables. Besides, the pilot probably spoke only Tagalog. He settled for "Whew."

Try as he might, Ben couldn't move the fear of death from his mind. He briefly closed his eyes, but the premonition remained—if this flight didn't kill him, it was leading to something that would. His friend Teddy, back in the States, set great store by premonitions. "Feelin's" he called them, and not to be ignored. Ben wasn't sure Teddy was right, but the chance that he might be on to something made his teeth chatter. In an effort to regain control, he forced himself to breathe deeply and very slowly.

His composure returned, and Ben noticed an old Filipina sitting quietly across from him. Head bowed piously, she was working a long string of rosary beads. He watched her smile and raise the small crucifix to her lips, a kiss he knew meant the end of her prayer.

Ben envied her faith. His own was currently in short supply. He was glad he wasn't wearing his collar, or any other sign of his vocation, because someone might ask him to pray. Right now Ben wasn't sure prayer could bring night after day, much less deliverance from harm. His mother, he knew, never had such doubts.

After World War II, like thousands of other Filipinas, Remedios Abarquez had married a lonely, lovestruck American soldier. Albert Lucero, Ben's father, was a lifer. This meant, for the Luceros, a series of drab assignments to bases in drabber army towns Stateside.

Remedios hated the disruptions of army life. For several years in America, she took refuge in the past and memories of home. And Ben, her first-born, became her primary audience, her ally in exile, and the child closest to her heart—a bond strengthened by earlier miscarriages. For him she painted vivid pictures—friends, relatives, places—and Ben imagined the people and places Remedios held so dear. And because he loved her, Cebu became his home as well.

For Ben, especially when he was very young, the notion that Cebu was home steadied him. It was a nice refuge, a haven from the uncertainties of continuing adjustments. His fantasy was also fed by Remedios's letters from relatives and by stacks of Philippine magazines and newspapers, all written in English. The latter he unbundled to read and re-read, so much so that he knew, before he reached age ten, the star personalities in the gossipy world of Philippine journalism, a world of politics and movies, boxers and beauty queens.

As Remedios became more Americanized, her stories about Cebu dwindled and eventually stopped. They had resumed a month or so ago, on the day marking the end of the year of mourning for Ben's father's death.

The family, scattered and grown now, was gathered at the parents' house. And it was then that Remedios announced she was ready to die. Ben's younger brothers and sisters—there were five in all—rushed forward, humoring her. Remedios seemed otherwise well, but Ben wasn't so sure. She wanted, she said, to be buried at home. And home was Cebu. There was enough money for travel and expenses and, she added, Ben would take her coffin there.

Remedios spoke evenly as her children and grandchildren gathered around, urging her not to mean what she so clearly had said. Only Ben stood off and looked straight at Remedios. As a child he had learned his mother's giveaways, his guide to separating the jokes, of which there were many, from the facts.

After a moment he stepped back, unable to accept what he saw. She was serious. It was then he started to prepare for her death and the duties he would assume.

Ben was notified a week ago. The doctor, an old family friend, said Remedios died in her sleep. He tried to explain the intricacies of a heart valve that failed, and all the while Ben nodded without hearing much. He knew the real cause of her death.

Filipinos, his mother always said, particularly those of her generation, knew sorrow better than most. Many had died of broken hearts. For Ben that was good enough. It explained his mother's death and his place on a plane to a city he had never seen.

To the surprise of most, the old jet landed safely, bouncing hard on the rough runway before coming to a halt. The passengers and crew cheered, the pious among them adding multiple signs of the cross for good measure.

The flight had been perilous by any standard. Now, as the plane taxied toward the terminal, the storm seemed to double in force. The rain, now driven, resounded in the cabin like small rocks pelting against a thin tin roof.

Good luck so far, Ben thought, as he leaned back in his seat, tuning out the storm, his eyes closed. He inhaled deeply, touching his temples and forehead to blot the perspiration. In a few minutes the door would open and he'd dash from the ramp to the cover of the terminal. Before then, he just wanted to collect himself and focus on other matters.

Remedios's directions had been clear and simple. Two weeks before she died, she told Ben to get his passport. "Apply now," she said. "Tell them it's emergency. You'll get it in a week, maybe less." She also said that when she died he must call Cebu, specifically Clara, her oldest and best friend, their friendship dating from the hard years of the Japanese Occupation and before. "She'll know what to do."

His mother was right, about her death, about the passport (it came in six days), and also about Clara. Ben dutifully called Clara two hours after he learned Remedios had died. He left a message. Clara wasn't in, nor did she call back.

Two days later Ben received a phone call from an airlines representative advising him to pick up a ticket he hadn't ordered—Seattle to Cebu via Manila. It was at the United counter at Seattle-Tacoma International, and could he please bring proper I.D.? He shook his head slowly as he hung up— Aunt Clara.

Through the window Ben could see Clara standing at a cordoned-off entry to the Cebu terminal. She hadn't changed much since her last visit to the States years ago. She was standing beside a young boy in green fatigues who was carrying a rifle. He looked nervous, shifting his weight from one foot to the other. Ben knew that the soldier's job was to keep unauthorized civilians, such as Clara, away from his assigned area. But he also knew Clara hated regulations, particularly those applicable to her. He imagined the poor boy trying vainly to enforce the rules, with Clara responding that General or Senator So-and-So, or maybe even the president, would hear about this!

Ben had come to know Clara from her many visits to the Lucero home. To him she was just Aunt Clara, warm and generous, but he knew she had another side.

There was that time in Seattle when he was ten. Clara hailed a cab to take Ben and a younger sister to the zoo. At the end of the ride she was sure the driver had cheated her; she immediately raised the subject of the fare. The matter soon grew heated, then out of control.

Ben recalled the anger and his own terror. The cabbie was screaming "Chinese bitch!" and Clara, seated in the rear with the children, was applying a stranglehold Lou Thesz would have admired. Only the frightened sobs of Ben and his sister caught Clara's attention and, quite possibly, spared the cabbie's life.

When Remedios heard of the incident she was furious. She and Clara disappeared into a room for what seemed like hours. When they emerged, Clara's eyes were bloodshot and swollen from crying.

"It won't happen again," Remedios said simply. And it didn't, at least not around the children. But Ben had always suspected that the traits his aunt took pains to suppress—her temper and her imperial arrogance—were still there. Below him, in front of the terminal, was their latest manifestation. Clara stood erect, haughty, seemingly invulnerable, certainly unstoppable.

Eventually Ben had come to understand that his aunt was a predator except around the Luceros. Beside her was the most recent evidence of this—a young, nervous boy with a gun. A soldier was Aunt Clara's latest meal.

At the top of the passenger ramp leading to the tarmac, Ben stopped, stunned by the power of a monsoon. Nothing had prepared him for this. Seattle storms seemed mild by contrast, almost sedate. The wind pushed him to the side, forcing him to grab the handrail. Instinctively he thrust his free arm across his face, shielding himself from hammering rains that stung him and blurred his vision. It was a futile gesture. His best course was to run low and hard for the safety of the terminal fifty meters away.

Overhead the sky was darker than morning had a right to be. To Ben, nature now seemed belligerent and intimidating and, for the first time, he started to understand how such power, once released, could drive rational men to superstition.

The storm was unseasonal; nature in the Philippines was evidently capricious. Back home, his Filipino friends and relatives had told him not to worry, that the rains didn't come, didn't *really* come, until July or August, and that he was lucky. March was a good month for travel. They were wrong, and he silently cursed them as he ran toward the terminal.

Once inside the building Ben had barely stopped to wipe his face when he saw Aunt Clara moving toward him. She was walking, then running, and he knew what would come next.

"Benny!" she yelled. No matter that he was drenched, she hugged him tightly, rocking him from side to side. Ben was as stiff as the back of a wooden chair, but it wasn't from a lack of affection. He loved his aunt. To him she was kind, she was caring, and she was his mother's closest friend. It was just his nature to be reserved and controlled. Nothing like Aunt Clara. Aunt Clara was prone to loud and spontaneous displays of affection for Ben and his brothers and sisters. As a child, such displays had always embarrassed him, and now was no exception.

"Good to see you, Auntie," he said lamely, looking around to see if anyone was watching. No one was and he relaxed.

"Benny," she said again, as she released her grip to hold him at arm's length and stare into his eyes. Clara then started to cry.

"Everything's ready, Benny," she said softly. "Everything. I know what she wants. I chose the plot years ago. The schedule's fixed."

Clara paused, unable to continue.

"But I do you no good like this, Nephew," she said as she struggled to compose herself. "No good."

Clara breathed deeply before speaking. "Come with me," she said evenly, taking his arm. "You must get out of these clothes and rest. I've already talked to the priest, and two days from now will be OK.

"Come with me," Clara repeated, now pulling his arm. "Wet clothes; a cold's next. We should hurry."

"But Auntie," Ben protested as they headed toward the exit.

"Ever the good son, Benny," Clara said with a smile. "A good son.

"Don't worry," she added, "Remedios is in good hands. That's why we have these." As she spoke she snapped her fingers at a group of young men who, at the sound, ran back toward the plane and the casket it still carried.

"They'll take care of her," said Clara.

In Cebu, home for Clara was on Mango Avenue, where her big stucco house and its gardens were surrounded by a brick wall with an imposing wrought-iron gate. The gatekeeper, a small brown man, bowed toward Clara as her chauffeured Mercedes drove in.

Ben was too tired to notice. The drive from the airport had

made him drowsy. Jet lag was already setting in, its effect doubled by the exhausting fear on the flight from Manila.

During the ride, Ben kept insisting to Clara that he wasn't tired, outward manifestations notwithstanding. He had to stay awake, he said, to help his aunt prepare for the burial just two days away.

"You're a good boy," Clara said then, "but it's taken care of. This was your first flight, and you've no idea how tired you are.

"You must rest," she said firmly.

As the car entered the gate and approached the house, Clara turned toward Ben, who sat with her in the rear seat. As always, she was ready to say more, but this time she stopped before speaking.

"I'm not tired," Ben declared, now more slowly, as his body sagged against the car door.

I'll wake you," the voice said, "when it's time." It was maternal, familiar and warm, and slowly Ben responded, stirring slightly. He could feel the bed underneath, and the soft satin sheets against his body. His eyes, now open, adjusted to the dim light.

He was in a small room, alone. He wondered about the time and whether he had imagined the voice. A dream, he thought, but it didn't matter. Ben was tired. Fatigue had seeped into his bones, doubling their weight, making initiative doubtful and movement impossible.

He breathed deeply, then shut his eyes, comfortable that when the time came, Clara would wake him. She had said everything was taken care of, he told himself. Unlike before, that was fine with him.

He could feel the muscles in his face relax. His eyes stayed closed, even after effort was withdrawn. Once more he heard, or thought he heard, the voice.

"Benny," it said quietly, "you're a good boy.

"You're a good boy" the voice said again, this time more softly.

Then there was silence.

PART I

— 1 —

Cebu

A top a tiny and sparse brown knoll in the small town of Talisay to the south of Cebu City, Remedios Lucero was finally laid to rest. She was home after an absence of more than three decades, her American sojourn. The cemetery grounds were neatly kept, disturbed only by parallel lines of freshly dug Philippine dirt. As Ben, Clara, and a handful of relatives watched, the casket slowly disappeared. The mourners were oblivious to an unseasonal outburst of March rain.

On this sad day in this melancholy place, Ben pondered again the limits of prayer. His own could surely not raise the dead in this world, and perhaps not even protect in the next. The brief thought elicited an involuntary shudder. It was the influence, he guessed, of Clara, who stood next to him.

He turned to go and was quickly joined by Aunt Clara. Clara Natividad was not really his aunt, but she had always been Remedios's closest friend. Their friendship dated back to childhood in the pre-war Philippines.

"Shared the same clothes and, later, the same foxhole," he remembered his mother saying.

Unlike Remedios, Clara was cynical and tough. She was reputed to be one of the most powerful women in Philippine politics. Despite their differences, their years together and apart had purified their bond, leaving at the end love and respect and, for Clara, a deep sense of loss.

As Ben and Clara walked through the mud that the cemetery had become, they stopped briefly under the partial protection of an ornate Chinese headstone. Clara, sitting on the edge of a marble abutment, lit a cigarette.

"One thing I like about the Chinese," she said flatly. "They know how to bury their dead."

Ben did not respond.

"Ashes to ashes," she said sadly. "Even your mom."

"Maybe," he quietly replied.

Clara took one last drag from the cigarette before flinging it to the side. There, among the wet blades of grass, it flickered for a moment before dying.

She was a pretty woman, Ben thought—as pretty as his mom. Through his childhood years there had been special moments, full of pauses and dramatic gestures, when Clara would share with him the most intimate and important secrets. Now, like a colt before a storm, Ben felt the approach of just such a moment.

"Tell me, Benny," Clara said slowly. "What do you know?"

The vagueness of the question puzzled Ben. "What do you mean?"

"What did Remedios tell you?"

"About what?"

Clara stared at Ben, her gaze intense. "About life here during the war, about who your mom and I were, about meeting your father—what did she say?"

Ben shrugged his shoulders, unsure of his aunt's direction. "Not a lot," he said.

"I thought so," Clara sighed. "So much of her is here. And that's why she is buried in Cebu and not in the States. She was gone a long time, but this place is always home—at least when it counts—for people like your mom and me.

"I didn't think she'd talk about it," Clara continued. "It wasn't her way—'Better they don't know,' she'd tell me. There was a lot of evil here, and so she escaped. She wanted something better for when she'd someday have children."

Clara blinked hard. She did not want to weep. It took a few moments, but she managed to collect herself.

"It was for you," she said emphatically. "She didn't say as much, but I know it was for you—you and the other kids. That's why she left, and that's why she didn't tell you about the bad things here. I'm sure you heard about everything that was good, but there was another world we all lived in, and she wanted to protect you from it. I know that. It's just her.

"Now it's time," Clara said, "to round out her life. Despite the suffering and hatred, your mother stayed human.

"Maybe that's why I loved her," she added quietly.

"I know," Ben said. "Me too."

"Come," Clara said, as she stood and took Ben's arm. "Let's walk to town. A little rain doesn't scare me. I'll dismiss my driver and we'll talk more. Your mom and I kept no secrets from each other, and I'll keep none from you. I'll tell you what I know."

— 2 —

Clara and Remedios: Untold Tales

Ben learned much that afternoon, about Clara as well as Remedios. The war made Clara an orphan, but it also made her rich. In November 1946, a bit more than a year after Japan's surrender, a rich relative died suddenly and left no will.

Uncle Pabling was visiting one of his many rice fields outside Cebu City. On the road leading to one of the fields, he stepped on a land mine left over from the Occupation. During the war he had made a fortune selling fish, produce, and women to the Japanese. Clara had disliked Uncle Pabling even before the war, but she hated him for his collaboration with the enemy. Nevertheless, she donned a black veil and mourned in appropriate fashion over the pieces of her uncle that were found and placed in the casket.

Once his remains were buried and forgotten, Clara hired an accountant to compute the value of Pabling's estate, and an attorney to file the necessary papers. A month later, in what must have been record time, she was declared Pabling's sole heir.

The use or abuse of law was easier then. The war killed the judges, closed the courts, and destroyed legal records. In post-war Cebu, law's application was at best uneven, all of which favored Clara's case.

She knew the new judges, appointed by Philippine officials who accompanied the returning American soldiers. There was one judge in particular. Before the war, she had known him only as "Chino," a nickname derived from the Chinese shape of his eyes.

In those pre-war days he was a young attorney, just starting his practice in Cebu City. He lived modestly, renting a room from the parents of one of Clara's friends. One afternoon she had met him there at the house. He seemed nice enough, Clara thought, and handsome, but too old. Chino was then in his twenties, while she was still a teenager.

When the Japanese came, Chino had fled to his home on the nearby island of Negros and joined a guerrilla unit. Four years later he was a judge; they met again by accident in Cebu City. Clara was walking toward downtown, or what remained of it, and Chino was driving a jeep hard the other way. At first she paid him little attention, even as he turned his jeep around and honked at her from behind.

Clara turned and smiled. She recognized Chino immediately. He was still handsome, Clara thought, and she was out of her teens. Dinner followed that evening and the next, and at some point in between, Pabling's estate was settled.

Fortunately, Pabling had never married—it was rumored he was *bakla*—so she never had to confront the protestations of yelping offspring. Any other competitors had been driven from the province or into the ground by Japanese and American bombs and shells.

Clara knew that a relative might someday return and claim his or her rightful share, so she subverted that possibility. Once she was declared the sole heir—a declaration due largely to her uncommon good looks and judicious use of them—she converted all of Pabling's assets to cash. With a trunkload of money, she caught the next boat for Manila.

Clara arrived in Manila on December 23, 1946. Earlier that year, the Philippines had become independent. Yet it seemed to her a melancholy day. Neither the excitement of the new political era nor the festivity of the season could hide the impact of Japan's terrible sin.

For Clara, it was her first time in the city. She had survived the war and, by any measure, she was tough. Nevertheless, she was nearly undone by what she saw. Devastation was complete, or nearly so. She had loved Manila as a child, though she had seen it only through pictures. These she had committed to memory. She mourned the city's once-graceful skyline and broad, tree-lined boulevards, now gone or damaged beyond recognition. Far worse was the sight, never to be forgotten, of skeletal children scrambling like animals through garbage, searching for food that wasn't there.

The first night was hard. She rented a room in a small hotel by Manila Bay, and during the night Clara thought of returning to Cebu. But by morning she realized that the moonscape of postwar Manila was where she had to be. She had money; the Americans were leaving; and everyone else was starting from below scratch. Even at age twenty-four, Clara had a rare and valuable skill—the capacity to visualize. What she saw was a city on its way back, and along the way she saw Clara Natividad, aging gracefully—and making a peso or two.

The question of how was answered by the Americans. What

the soldiers could not carry with them, they left behind. And what they left—aside from war babies—was surplus equipment, jeeps in particular. Her Manila of the future would need cheap transportation, and Clara intended to meet that demand.

She stole her first jeep. Actually, she had it stolen from a young man who had stolen it earlier from the U.S. Army. She watched him intently over a period of weeks—from the time of acquisition, to the first coat of paint, to the dismantling of the machine gun mounted on the back. She never did the work; she had enough money to hire people. In those days, anyone could be hired very cheaply.

Clara purchased a house in Ermita, a district in the heart of Manila just east of the bay. In anticipation of her new venture, she rented a large warehouse in Makati—an outlying district miles from her residence. The cops—what cops there were—would never look there. She knew her time for freebooting was short, because the police and the city would eventually get organized. But by then she hoped to have made enough money to pay off anybody. As usual, Clara was right.

So every morning, she jumped in a taxicab with two or three of her employees and simply told the driver to drive. When she came across a jeep that had not been destroyed, she pointed it out to her associates for future reference. Even the ones that were little better than scrap were marked out. Spare parts, she said.

No jeep was safe. After a year of constant collection, warehousing, and repair, two of her fleet hit the streets of an unsuspecting Manila. The first, christened the "Doña Clara," was named for her; the second, the "Most Blessed Virgin," was not.

They were awful, convoluted things. Squat, small benches

that faced each other had been added in the back, while a low top covered it all. But what was impressive were the knockout colors—greens, yellows, and reds predominated.

The drivers started at dawn, choosing selected routes, and drove all day and most of the night. The people rode her jeepneys, and Clara got rich, very rich. For her, wealth meant diversification—smuggling, assorted vices, and politics. By 1950 she owned two senators and had a lease, with an option to purchase, on the president himself.

That was one side of Clara—Clara, the jaded survivor. The other remained intensely loyal to those she loved. For Clara Natividad, this mostly meant people she knew before her first day in Manila. She had loved few since then—not the men she slept with, nor the girls she sold, nor the politicians she owned. And the one person she loved most was Remedios Lucero, Ben's mother.

Remedios left the Philippines in June 1946, before Clara became wealthy. In late May Remedios met—or rather, her mother met—a dull but stable Filipino-American G.I. The details of an arranged marriage, common at the time, were quickly worked out between Aurelia Abarquez, Remedios's mother, and Albert Lucero, Aurelia's future son-in-law.

A lbert was neither handsome nor bright but, for Aurelia, these were good traits in her daughter's future mate. Since he was neither, she figured he would never, could never, cheat on her baby. It had been almost a year since Japan surrendered, but Albert was still in uniform and gave no indication of ever taking it off.

"I'll be buried in it," Albert declared proudly.

"Stability and America," Aurelia murmured to herself.

When Aurelia advised her daughter of her impending marriage, Remedios protested without success. In such disputes,

Aurelia always cited tradition—which, in this case, favored arranged marriages—and always won. Cited also was a fact Remedios could not contest.

"You're getting old," Aurelia said. "You're almost twenty-four."

Remedios sadly hung her head. For the passing of time, she had no reply.

The wedding was held in the remnants of a church. The bride made an effort to look gay, but the best she could manage was a glassy-eyed stare at nothing in particular. It was the look of the refugee, except set in lace.

Clara stood in the back and cried real tears—not the false variety she later forced at Pabling's funeral. That wedding day was the last time she felt real sorrow—a sense of true loss—until 1983 when Remedios died.

Until then, they corresponded constantly. And since Clara had money, she visited twice yearly while the children were growing up, staying at the best hotel in whatever army town Albert was stationed. She was always invited to the Lucero home, but she always declined, saying she didn't want to impose. The truth was that she could barely tolerate Albert, whom she would sarcastically salute—Nazi-style—behind his back.

Clara was there at the birth of all five of the Lucero children. Naturally, she became a godmother, which is not odd, to all of them—which is. Clara insisted.

And Aunt Clara loved them all. But her favorite was Ben, the first-born, because she saw more of Remedios in him. There's something special about first-borns, particularly those of immigrants. Although born in the new land, their earliest lessons are the ones from home.

Clara knew that Ben was his mother's young confidant during her first lonely years away from Cebu. In Clara's regard, this made him the golden one, and she made little effort to conceal her bias. She wasn't a parent, so she never had to worry about familial equality or harmony.

On one occasion Clara volunteered a promise: she would raise Ben if anything should happen to Remedios; her sense of *utang*, obligation, demanded no less. Remedios thanked her friend for her concern, but quietly remarked that Albert might have a say in determining Ben's future.

Clara, clearly disappointed, would never mention it again. But at the time she could not resist muttering that Albert's talent was limited to polishing his army boots and marching, not raising Ben.

It was obvious that she saw nothing of the father in the son. Ben, she said many a time to Remedios, was going somewhere —"to the top!"—wherever the top might be. "And Reming," Clara would say excitedly, "when he's old enough—I mean, if it's OK *na lang*—he can come to the Philippines and manage my business.

"I'll even pay him U.S. money," Clara added emphatically. Among Filipinos, U.S. money was never taken lightly. It was the ultimate weapon of persuasion.

In appropriate response, Remedios would widen her eyes, nod her head, and appear to agree. But she did not. The boy belonged to God. Her first-born would be a priest.

Manila is a city of night. Six in the morning is twilight and contrast—when the young and the rich are stumbling in and everyone else is preparing to stumble out. As was her custom, Clara watched it all from her veranda. Seated, she sipped her coffee and glanced at the morning paper. It was September 20, 1964, and a small item hidden on the society page happened to catch her eye.

It featured a woman she once knew, years ago, in harder days. Now, the woman was the aggressive wife of a rising young politician. At one of the many Manila social functions, this suddenly prim lady gave an address on the state of the city.

"Tourists will not come," she began, "to a Manila they fear." The first step in her proposed plan was to close establishments that catered to prurient interests.

"Then *puta*," Clara snorted at the paper, "close your legs. I remember when you slept for your lunch."

It was not as if the moralist's proposal posed any great personal threat. It did not. Clara Natividad had long since outgrown catering to men's needs. It was more a matter of principle—one of the few she had—that vice and virtue should be out and on the table, visible to all who cared to see.

The only exception to her outspoken bluntness was in her relationship with Remedios and the children. Because of them, she tolerated Albert, but just barely.

Roman, Clara's servant of long standing, knew his mistress well. And his servant's wisdom told him that when she was this way, it was best to wait. So he waited patiently in the darkness of the adjoining room, a fresh pot of coffee in one hand and a letter in the other.

Finally Clara threw down the paper in disgust and lit up a cigarette. Outside, Roman counted. After the tenth ring of smoke crawled slowly past Clara's forehead, he approached her cautiously.

"Would you like more coffee, Ma'am?"

He knew there would be no response. There never was. It was an old game, and they both knew the rules. Perpetual pro forma. She always liked a second cup, so he poured, as usual, and placed the letter discreetly on the table by the silverware.

It was from the States.

"Roman," Clara said sharply. "Why didn't I get this yesterday?"

"You weren't here yesterday, Ma'am."

Which was true, and Clara knew it. So she shut her mouth, smiled, and eagerly opened the letter. It was from Remedios.

Letters from Remedios always began the same way "The kids are fine, as is Albert (who received another promotion)."

It was the same format—almost a copy of past letters that Clara had received. And every time Albert was promoted, she knew it was for endurance rather than for talent.

"And Ben spent his first day in the seminary."

That line sat there near the bottom of the page, just above the last sentence, which briefly mentioned the youngest girl's polio shot. Innocuous stuff, really.

Not really. Clara screamed.

Why, Remedios? Why? Why the Church? Don't you remember that everything died the day the Japanese came? They killed and we ran. But they caught you, dear girl. . . and now you wish to pass it on. . . ?

The Church and the God it represented had failed Clara. In the end, she had prayed over too many dead brothers, parents, and friends. Prayer, she later concluded, had never saved her, while a good eye and selective cruelty had. It was not a matter of dramatic revelation; the loss of faith is seldom a conscious process. Rather, it was simply that one day the shooting stopped, while the numbness in her heart continued.

Before the war, Clara and Remedios had been young girls, then young women together, as close as young girls and young women could be, which is something most men cannot begin to fathom. From the first grade through high school, they had been classmates. Over the years they had come to trust each other fully, exchanging favors and courtesies as well as secrets of varied import.

In the process they became sisters, or at least it seemed that way. Actually they were closer than sisters, because their friendship, unlike ties of blood, was freely entered and consciously nurtured and maintained.

When the Japanese invaded Cebu, Clara and Remedios fled the city, their parents insisting that they leave. There were rumors of what the Japanese did to women, particularly young women such as they.

They walked, then ran toward the western edge of town, where the wooded hills began. Once there, they followed a narrow path that wound gradually upward. Clara, the stronger of the two, took the lead. Remedios fell in behind. As they walked, Remedios kept falling farther behind, exhausted by her friend's brisk pace. On two occasions, Clara stopped and turned toward Remedios, allowing her to catch up before setting off once more.

She stopped and turned a third time, only to see her friend disappear behind a stand of trees. Then Clara heard rough male shouts—and Remedios's single desperate scream telling Clara to run.

Clara ran straight ahead, but not too far, a hundred meters or so, just off the trail. She hoped the brush was thick enough to hide her because she knew the Japanese would come this way. She waited, not moving, not even breathing too hard.

Finally, approaching footfalls—then much nearer. Five soldiers were walking single file. Remedios, gagged and in the middle, had her hands tied behind her. After the fifth soldier passed, Clara followed, hiding and watching. It was late afternoon and night would soon fall. Eventually, she knew, they would stop. It was then she planned to make her move.

Long after night fell, Clara waited and watched at the edge of a small abandoned village. Among the banyans she was invisible and still. The Japanese had pitched camp hours ago, but she dared not move. To her right, less than twenty meters away, was the hut in which they were keeping Remedios. Although a lantern hung outside the entry, the feeble light it produced was no match for the jungle night.

The soldiers were drunk. They had found several jars of *tuba*, the local wine. All five of them were there. Clara could count their shadows from her vantage point.

They stood single file outside the hut, passing the jar around. In turn, the one closest to the door would enter and exit some minutes later. They reminded Clara of young children at school, lined up patiently and waiting for candies, fruits, and other treats.

Clara listened for Remedios. She thought she heard her scream once, after the first soldier disappeared into the hut. Then there was nothing except rough laughter and a harsh language she did not understand.

It was just before dawn when the shadows stopped moving, and the sounds of the jungle replaced the slurred conversations. The *tuba* had taken effect. Clara knew its potency, having drunk a bottle down by the stream the year before.

She emerged from among the trees and moved cautiously toward the building. Four of the sleeping soldiers were dispersed in different corners of the small clearing. These she avoided easily. But she knew there were five, and the fifth one would not be so fortunate.

Their weapons and ammunition belts had been placed against the side of the hut. They expected no danger here.

She unsheathed a bayonet from one of the belts and, silent and barefoot, ascended the stairway. The fifth soldier was on the landing, passed out. He lay face up on the wooden floor, mouth open, a fine, unbroken line of saliva moving slowly down his left cheek.

He was just a boy, slightly older than Clara, and rather handsome, Clara thought, for a Japanese.

She knelt down beside him, the bayonet clasped firmly in her right hand. Simultaneously, she placed her free hand over his mouth and plunged the blade through the hollow of his throat, between the Adam's apple and breast bone. She buried the blade to the hilt, twisting it violently. The tip pierced the thin floorboard, impaling the soldier like a mounted insect specimen.

It was quiet, efficient, and easy. His body convulsed, but other than that, there was no sound. She watched him for a remorseless moment, then turned her attention elsewhere.

Remedios was sitting in the corner of the dim room, her small body upright, rocking slowly, her knees hugged tightly against her chest. She saw it all but said nothing. What remained of her clothing, she had wrapped—or attempted to wrap—around herself. She looked at Clara dully, giving no recognition of what had transpired.

Clara touched her hand gently, held it, and crooned a little girl's song they both knew. Gently she helped her friend to her feet and down the stairway. It was clear Remedios could not walk very far or very fast, and so Clara carried her piggyback style, past the soldiers, into the jungle, and toward the mountains where they would spend the rest of the war.

N o one, as yet, has been able to explain the paradox of faith and its relationship to tragedy—why cruelty and death can sometimes reclaim the hardest case, while, at the same time, can lose the heart of the truest believer. Are humans so weak that they need to believe in something—anything—other than themselves, and will even worship conjecture if it is passably presented? Or does an arbitrary living God choose His believers, selecting a few while condemning the majority?

These two unpleasant notions coexist, as do the effects of tragedy, sometimes in contrast, but often in sharp and painful contradiction. In times of peace, the distinctions between contrast and contradiction may blur as answers to questions seem unimportant. But because of war, the hard questions can live like memories of the jungle in the minds of survivors, long after the last bullet's discharge.

And the questions were there in the Philippines the day MacArthur came ashore at Leyte. MacArthur meant survival and an eventual end to the tragedy. But the simple fact of survival meant different things to different people. This was true even for two who were closer than sisters.

For Clara, survival was owing to a number of factors, none of which was even remotely linked to God.

For Remedios, however, survival reaffirmed her faith in the religion of her childhood. It wasn't as if she had spent the Occupation years in prayer and seclusion. She had not. Remedios had shot enemy soldiers, tortured prisoners, and executed Japanese wounded as eagerly as any male guerrilla. Yet, despite the savagery of her existence, when she heard that MacArthur had landed, she knelt and prayed her thanks, crossing and recrossing herself in Catholicism's universal sign.

Ultimately, for Remedios Lucero, survival meant that God would save. He would test but never abandon His children, and Douglas MacArthur was His indelible sign.

What do you do with believers? Historically, if believers professed antagonistic creeds, the more powerful sect inevitably characterized the weaker one as infidels. In doing so, they denied them the validity of their creed. This was the first step toward their eradication. Without a creed, infidels became less than human. They could be disposed of like carp in a pond. The syllogism roughly followed this line: Humans have creeds; infidels do not. Infidels, therefore, are not human.

Amazing, isn't it, how that perverse logic transcends culture and time, finding common ground among Christians, Muslims, and political ideologues. A question of not having a creed? No. It's more a matter of not having the proper creed at the proper time. "Believer" and "infidel" ought to stand in stark contrast. Instead the terms are interchangeable, useless, proposing to connote so much but actually defining very little. In the postwar Philippines—as on every other former battleground—there was room for both.

Remedios, ostensibly the believer, believed in God; Clara, undoubtedly the infidel, believed in herself. God, she thought, had done her no good. It was not as if Clara disbelieved. She did not. She simply refused to honor the God of the Occupation. So she turned mostly inward, to herself, to someone she knew and trusted.

"God," she told Remedios on the latter's last Sunday in Cebu, "is a cruel bastard. He's worse than the Japanese because they didn't owe us anything. And you're a pious fool, with your cotton dress and your black rosary beads. Where was God when the soldiers took you to the hut? Was He watching it? Did He enjoy it? Fool!"

The statement, both for its anger and its substance, shocked Remedios. She had simply asked Clara to walk with her to the church, not to attend the service. Remedios knew that Clara, even before the war, was no great practicing Catholic. Remedios did not mind. All she wanted was a moment with a friend. But what she got was a diatribe, sharper than a slap.

She flushed as she felt the rush of blood upward, heating,

ever so lightly, the lobes of both ears. For an instant the two women glared at each other—speechless across a sudden gulf where one false move could shape eternity, preclude forgiveness, and mean, in essence, the end of it all.

Clara, sensing the edge and the pit below, pulled back first.

"I'm sorry," she said quickly, averting her eyes. She turned and walked away, mumbling something about "tomorrow."

Remedios stood quietly and watched her friend depart. She could feel her anger gradually subside, and she knew the color of her face was returning to normal. She also knew that Clara never apologized, so that her hasty phrase of contrition was more than even a sister could expect.

The church bell clanged rudely in the remnants of the old parish steeple. It was an odd sound, a bit off. Like so many other things in Cebu, the bell had survived the war but just barely, losing a chunk of itself in the process. The tower that had given it resonance had been substantially destroyed. The Japanese had used it as a sniper post, and the Americans had dispatched both sniper and tower in equal portions.

Only the skeletal structure remained, supporting a bell that now seemed too large. But it rang today, as it had rung before the war, and that was what mattered.

On this, her last Sunday in Cebu, Remedios felt a particularly keen need for God's help. She was leaving for the States on Monday, tomorrow. On the morning of their wedding, Albert had received orders to report Stateside. He left Cebu by ship two days later, leaving behind a stranger who was also his wife. He promised to send for her after he reported to his new assignment—Fort Ord in northern California—and found suitable housing. A month passed and then another, and there was no word. The more time that passed, the happier Remedios became. Her mother, Aurelia, grew alarmed by the silence and urged her daughter to pray harder, unaware that when Remedios prayed, it was not for word from abroad.

Finally, earlier that week, a steamship ticket arrived from the U.S., an event prompting different reactions from mother and daughter. Aurelia screamed and laughed like she had found a bar of gold in her bed or, better still, had lived sufficiently long to see an aging daughter well married. For Remedios, the ticket's arrival marked the start of a time full of sadness, introspection, and a large dose of despair.

As she walked slowly that Sunday morning down the dirt road toward the church, she tried to resign herself to her fate. God, she told herself, would provide, and because He would, everything would somehow be for the better.

The thought brought her comfort. She stopped and, with eyes closed, whispered, "I accept," before moving on.

Comforting also was the thought of seeing Clara tomorrow, to say goodbye and to heal what hurts remained.

"Tomorrow," she said softly as she made her way, now more quickly down the road.

"Tomorrow."

As usual, a crowd gathered to see the travelers off—the usual assortment of friends and relatives, but most were just people with nothing to do. In slow, small Cebu, anything—even a ragged steamer—passed for entertainment.

The old steamer, the *Santo Kristo*, lay secured to the pier. The water was calm, in direct contrast to the activity on the dock. The boat had seen decades of inter-island service and had had several owners. Each decade or so it was renamed. The *Santo Kristo* had started service as the *Visayan Princess*. At midlife it had become the *Santa Lucia* and, eventually, the *Magdalena*. The last five years had seen it evolve from the

Magdalena to the *Santa Maria*, and finally, to the *Santo Kristo*, switching, in the last instance, gender as well as name. In the course of a lifetime, the old Princess had gone past the secular through ascending levels of the sacred, as if it anticipated (or its owners anticipated) the inevitable and resolved to take no chances.

Backing up the gangplank, Remedios waved at her relatives and friends while pretending to smile. Stopping in the middle, she began to wave furiously, hoping to catch a glimpse of Clara. Other passengers crowded quickly by her. Finally, uneasily, she stood there alone, all others having boarded.

A sudden sense of exile—even of abandonment—triggered what might have been one small, involuntary tear. If it was, and if it fell, it blended quickly with the thin film of perspiration on her upper cheek. For the crowd, or anyone else, there was never a tear—just a lady with a smile, waving a bit slower now.

"Mu'm," a voice interrupted. Remedios looked up. It was a crewman on the ship's side.

"We're an hour behind, Mu'm, and Manila's twenty-four hours away."

She shrugged, and silently turned toward the voice. On board, she chose a cot on the upper deck by the stern. Her neighbor was an old Filipino with two live chickens in a basket.

"Inday," the old man asked, *"asa ka?"*

"To Manila, *Manong*." English, she figured, would be her new language, and she had better get used to it.

The old man, upon hearing a response, was eager to talk. But the engines started, drowning out his efforts and granting Remedios her respite.

She stood alone at the stern and leaned on the railing. As she watched quietly, the brown skins on the dock blended into white and the other soft cotton colors until there was just the green outline of an island she once knew.

The next month of Remedios's life passed as a single unit of time—like an hour or a day. Years later, one of her children asked what the voyage was like. And she replied that, for the most part, she could not recall.

The human eye cannot measure the ocean, and since it cannot, it accepts a lesser truth. Accordingly, time does not exist there, or if it does, it does so uneasily.

For Remedios, the ocean had packed her days together, reducing her world to two constants—her cabin and a feeling of perpetual motion. It was a safer world—far safer, she felt, than the one she was about to enter.

That block of time, with a beginning and an end, had few features in between. She did recall disembarking in Manila and boarding a U.S.–bound freighter. She also remembered her arrival in San Francisco, what she saw and felt.

It was evening, and on the dock stood Albert in his soldier's suit, with a smile that reflected either a child's innocence or a fool's confusion.

Again, she was on a gangplank. It seemed her recent realities ended and began on gangplanks—in precarious suspension between two worlds. Again, passengers moved briskly by her, merging with the anonymous activity on the dock.

The busy hum below grew more faint as other travelers and those who welcomed them edged slowly away from the waterside, becoming figments of the shrouded night—anonymous, insignificant, unreal. Finally, there were only two.

Staring at Albert, who was forty feet away, she remained immobile and unsure. Through it all, he stood resolutely smiling, hands firmly in his pockets, collar upturned, in a futile attempt to resist the chill fog of San Francisco's early evening.

The coat enveloped Albert, almost overwhelming him. He seemed much too small. The contours of his face disappeared behind the great collar and the thickening mist.

Between the uneven thrusts of the oncoming fog, she glimpsed the fixed smile. It was slightly odd but not ominous, since Albert evoked indifference rather than fear. To her eyes, he was simply very unattractive. As he stood there, she swore he resembled a tree stump with teeth.

The thought of marriage to such a man was just too much. Remedios Lucero—who had survived the brutalities of the Occupation, abandonment by Clara, and the absence of everything dear and familiar—lost it all.

It started innocently enough—a sneeze and a shiver—but it became a caterwaul of symphonic proportions. She draped the top half of her body over the gangplank railing and howled like a mad, wounded beast. The howls were interspersed with sobs which at first were tearless, because pain had somehow been severed from remorse. But that night on the gangplank, the link was about to be re-established.

In the course of a woman's life, the tears of adolescence are perhaps the most profuse and surely the most confusing. But Remedios had had no adolescence. In her life there had been no confusion—simply vengeance and survival.

As the first solitary tear escaped the corner of an eye, she paused momentarily, surprised by a tiny presence both foreign and forgotten. She couldn't remember the last time she really cried. Was it at the dock at Cebu? Or before the war?

She was aware of the tear's course. It moved slowly down her face, touching upon arid points of passion and sorrow. Others followed. Some were shed retroactively for sadness felt but never expressed. Others were for a future that promised a poor return for sacrifice rendered. Remedios Lucero was twenty-four years old.

The distinction at first was lost on Albert as he watched his wife from the dock, his hands thrust deeply into the pockets of his long soldier's coat. At first he was stunned. Perhaps she was sick? She wore only a cotton print wholly out of place in the chill of this San Francisco night.

But as she continued to cry, he seemed at first to shrink a bit beneath the upturned collar, showing even less to those who cared to look. He began to feel embarrassed and angry. He turned to walk off the dock; then suddenly he stopped.

"The least I can do," he muttered.

Grim-faced, he returned to the gangplank. But as he approached his wife, the rectitude of his stride lessened. He paused before ascending the narrow runway; he lowered the flaps of his protective collar. If Remedios had chanced to look, she would have seen a changed face—still confused and sad, but far softer.

Albert quickly unfastened his coat and placed it gently on her shoulders. Standing back like a soldier on review, he was careful not to touch her.

Remedios turned slowly toward her husband. Glancing up, she saw him motion for her to follow him off the gangplank. Without thinking, she rose stiffly and walked to the edge of the pier.

There, under the opaque luster of the ship's bow lights, husband and wife silently confronted each other. The coat, far too large for Albert, devoured Remedios as it hung loosely from her shoulders. Her head bowed, she seemed to seek shelter within the darkness of the great woolen cape.

She had no words for this man who stood three feet from her, arms folded firmly across his soldier's chest. She was grateful for the protection—however temporary—that the coat provided. In this foreign land, it was her only solace. But even the guarantee of government issue did not protect fully, as the rapidly plunging temperature evoked from her a slight shiver, and from him a response of uncommon grace.

It was his nature. Albert, a man of limits, had never been good with words. He was, as a former grade school teacher described him, insufficiently clever. So he adjusted, substituting compassion, good humor, and later, courage, for what he was born without and could never acquire.

Arguments of brighter classmates eluded him. Sophistries and syllogisms bounced like drops of rain off his broad Filipino back. He never understood the language, nor did he care to. His concerns were more basic and, in a real sense, perhaps more accurate.

A shudder—like football or death—was something concrete, prompting, in turn, his response. In his world, it was language of sorts, and that was enough.

Bridging what seemed to him an infinite gap, he knelt in front of Remedios. Rising slowly, he fastened the buttons of the great coat.

"There," he said as he finished his task and stepped back once more.

"You know," he said evenly, "I even thought it might work. 'Arrange marriage, good Filipina girl,' Dad said. 'Your only chance.' So I did, and it don't work. Can't blame you."

Remedios was taken aback, but she heard no anger in his voice. She was not sure what to expect next, least of all the smile that reappeared. It was gentle and foolish, and wholly out of place.

"You know, I just got paid. Got some money in the bank. Uncle Sam don't pay much, but at least it's steady. I'll getcha place to stay, and somethin' to eat. Tomorrow we'll see an agent for your ticket back home.

"Hey, what can you say?"

As he spoke, he shrugged his shoulders Filipino-style. She

recognized it immediately. It was his way of showing resignation, a concession to fate and its superior, arbitrary powers.

Remedios was safe and she knew it. Yet that knowledge brought no relief. She was touched, lightly and uncomfortably so, by this odd and unexceptional little man.

"Come on," he said, interrupting her reverie. "We'd better get goin'."

To the handful of stevedores on the dock or the occasional pair of lovers, they must have seemed a strange sight. Albert strode manfully toward the fence beyond the pier, while Remedios—hampered by the constraints of the coat—waddled like a penguin. If, when they walked, they were not quite together, they were also not fully apart.

Finally, they reached their destination, disappearing behind the glare of dual headlights and the start of an automobile engine.

It was her first night in America.

PART II

— 3 —

The Toledo Road

Cebu is a flat city surrounded by rolling hills and a bay. Uphill to the west, a narrow, meandering road cuts through a sparse, stringy forest on its way to Toledo, another seaport town.

At the start of the road to Toledo squatted an old man— maybe sixty—and two slightly younger companions. They boarded the bus, which was packed with humans, cargo, and assorted animals, and remained silent as the coach ground its way up the dirt path toward its destination.

Half an hour, then an hour passed. As the altitude increased, so too did the chatter of the passengers. People were glad to escape Cebu's tropical swelter. But the three sat silently as they gazed at the valley below.

The old man loved these hills. During the Occupation, they had nurtured and protected him from the enemy. He was strong, young, and fast then, but his wife and his brother were not. They died in the valley, shot in the back as they ran from the Japanese.

At the side of this road, near a point the bus was now round-ing, he had last seen his mother and father. They were too old for war and too weak from hunger. The Japanese caught them too.

"There wasn't time," he once sadly recalled to Loloy, who now sat beside him. "The patrol came too fast." When the danger passed, he returned. But his parents were gone.

Carlito was sad, but he felt he had been a good son. Later, he became a good father, despite his propensity for bars and an occasional affair. And as a grandfather, he doted shame-lessly on his three *apo*—two boys and a girl. At that time, his earlier sins seemed not to have followed him. The proof of this was the children. They were handsome—neighbors kept re-minding Carlito (he never lost the childhood "-ito" despite his advancing years)—and he would beam with justifiable pride.

Malnutrition, cruelest to the young, was a stranger in the home of his *apo*. Carlito saw to that. The dark angel always passed over, leaving the bloated bellies and hollow eyes to be worn by the grandchildren of others.

Carlito's girl, in particular, was beautiful—soft black eyes, dark brown hair, a bit taller than most, with mahogany skin that made him smile a gap-toothed, gilded smile. Now she was dying. Three months ago the doctors at the Chinese hospital in Cebu had told him so. Leukemia, one doctor said, as the other solemnly nodded. "There's not much that can be done," the talkative one added, "not even in the States, much less here. *Walay mahimo, Manong, anugon lang.*" Again, the others nodded.

Wordless, Carlito had turned and left. He neither screamed nor argued; it was not his way. Instead he shook his head sadly and walked straight ahead. He knew his obligation. "*Mahimo man,*" he said quietly as he walked out the hospital's side door. "*Mahimo man.*"

The memory of his *apo's* suffering jolted him now as the bus lurched around the bend at the highest point on the road to Toledo. From here it would be downhill toward the sea with no scheduled stops—because the brakes were almost gone. In an emergency, should one arise, the driver could stop by strategically downshifting and selectively stroking the brake as he would a lover.

For Carlito, now was an emergency. *"Bay, diri, diri!"* he screamed from his seat. Gesturing wildly, his two companions joined in. The enormous cacophony of the three drew startled glances from villagers walking in the opposite direction.

"Pastilian bay!" the astonished driver exclaimed as he jammed the brake pedal clear to the floor. The old bus, unused to such a forceful command, shimmied and shook like a homely Manila table dancer substituting enthusiasm for talent and beauty.

Sometimes it works. To everyone's surprise, the bus did stop, metal on metal notwithstanding. Carlito and his friends then picked their way gingerly through the sudden free-for-all in the aisle—bawling children, disheveled mothers, and distraught poultry.

Once out of the bus, Carlito led the others away from the road toward a small thicket of trees. He paused at the edge of the woods, staring straight ahead at the trunk of the largest tree in the cluster. He stood unmoving, seeming not to breathe, as beads of sweat formed slowly on his temples and the bridge of his nose. A trickle of blood broke from Carlito's left nostril, cresting briefly on his thick upper lip before continuing downward.

Carlito's companions watched him, transfixed, and given their superstitious ways, more than a little afraid. Possession? By what or whom? It happened here often, even to priests. Loloy, who was older and had known Carlito longer, had never seen him like this. He broke the silence with great hesitation. *"Manong,"* he said, his voice barely above a whisper. At times like this, full of foreboding and dread, God and the spirits (Loloy took no chances and worshipped both) should not be disturbed by loud talk or rude noises. *"Manong,"* he repeated more firmly, emboldened by the apparent lack of otherworldly retribution.

At the second *"Manong,"* Carlito shuddered and seemed himself again. *"Kapoy,"* he said shaking his head wearily, *"'sus ka kapoy nako."* The sound of Carlito's voice comforted Loloy and Cacoy. "Come," Carlito then said in perfect English, which they had never heard him use before. "Come, my friends, we have work to do."

Both were unnerved, particularly Cacoy, whose first inclination was to break for the road and run to Cebu. But after Cacoy's initial uneasiness, which was stifled by a hard look from Loloy, old habits prevailed. Carlito was their leader. They would follow him dutifully, as always, even though nothing was the same.

Carlito moved quickly through the maze of undergrowth and trees. He avoided branches that seemed to strike only the two that followed. Their curses could be heard even if one stood by the road's edge, as a small group of the curious were now doing. *"Walay utok,"* said one old man sadly with a shake of his head, shuffling away as the group slowly dispersed. He had lived near the road's edge almost seventy years now. He knew that since the days of the invaders, what the forest took in was not readily surrendered. The forest was hallowed because bloodshed will sanctify, and during the Occupation so much blood was spilled it was said to have colored the ground, giving it a reddish hue that not even the monsoons nor the passage of time and the erosion of memory could erase.

— 4 —

Vengeance

The Occupation—a name and a period of time that Filipinos will never forget. When said aloud, it has almost an Old Testament resonance; when said in conjunction with adjoining names and periods—the Invasion, the Occupation, the Liberation—only the deliberately deaf can miss the parallel.

During the Occupation, the Japanese soldiers had terrorized the people by the road to Toledo. For every soldier killed nearby in a guerrilla ambush, the Japanese had repaid in kind. Even children were taken, and one afternoon, when the sun was hottest, the villagers were gathered and forced to watch in horror as a newborn child was grabbed from the arms of his mother by an unsmiling Korean sergeant. The Korean—whose stocky, neckless build distinguished him from the smaller Japanese—threw the screaming infant perhaps forty feet into the air. He raised his rifle and tracked the descent as Lou Gehrig might have followed a pop fly in Yankee Stadium. At the last second, he thrust upward with the attached bayonet, piercing the child through the breast.

"There," he said through a hooded interpreter as he brought the rifle forward and presented the baby to its mother. "He's dancing on the tip."

"Execution," he called it, naming the unnameable. The horror was multiplied beyond counting by the carnage in the woods. There, captured guerrillas and villagers suspected of aiding them were taken and were herded into a clearing. They were beaten and then executed, their bodies left where they had fallen. At times, particularly during the summer months of March and April, the stench carried for miles, mixing with the dust from the road, settling like a malevolent pollen upon those still living.

The smell did not leave, not even after the Americans returned and the executions had stopped when everyone understood that the war was about to end. But comprehension and acceptance are, as they have always been, distinct and different things. For the Japanese, in the Philippines and all through the Pacific, the fighting would continue. Ironically, this continuance pleased some Filipinos; vengeance motivated them when love could not. The guerrillas on Cebu became increasingly bold as news of MacArthur's successes reached the Philippines. Insurgent attacks grew larger and were launched with greater frequency, and while the guerrillas suffered more casualties, so too did the Japanese.

Sitoy's Story

After one successful ambush on the road to Toledo, the guerrillas inspected the bodies of the dead and dying soldiers, pilfering cigarettes, watches, and an occasional ring, along with the weapons and ammunition of the fallen. One guerrilla, a boy no older than thirteen, went from body to body, kicking each one in the ribs, waiting to hear a telltale sound or see a twitch. If there was either, he would put a round in the back of the neck or, if the soldier was on his back and was too heavy to move, the target was the forehead.

The boy had already shot two survivors and approached a third, who was lying on his side, curled like a fetus. Sitoy could see his arm move, a sign of life which, on the Toledo Road, sealed his death.

Sitoy kicked him hard on the shoulder, the impact forcing the body on its back. The soldier moaned, and Sitoy studied him closely for a moment before aiming his gun. He wore a sergeant's insignia, but the boy knew he wasn't Japanese; his thick neck and stocky build gave him away. A Korean, he thought, as he felt his index finger gently touch the trigger.

Among Filipinos, the Koreans had developed a reputation for a strain of senseless cruelty even greater than that of the Japanese. Subjects of Japan, they sought to please their masters. Savoring this execution, Sitoy paused before pulling the trigger.

"*Huwat!*" barked a voice, commanding him to stop. Reluctantly, he did so.

Because of his age, he had very little standing and was not allowed to argue, much less disobey. Three years earlier, Sitoy was the sole survivor of a Japanese sweep through his village in the northern corner of the valley. He was adopted by a guerrilla patrol that found him bleeding through a hole in his throat.

Slowly, he recovered his health, all but his ability to speak. In the Filipino way, Sitoy owed his life to his saviors, and his *utang* to them would never end. As soon as he recovered, he requested combat because he saw it as a way to start repaying his debt. But his requests, made through an improvised sign language, were always denied. He was too young, he was told, and the weapons were too few. What weapons they had were for prospects more promising than he.

And so, Sitoy learned to cook and to bandage the wounded—there was need for both—and partly as a reward and partly out of need, he was eventually allowed to accompany the patrols. Sitoy was gunless at first—captured weapons still went to others—but that ended after a successful ambush near Mandaue, a small barrio on the edge of Cebu City. The trap was particularly well laid; the small enemy detachment was wiped out during the initial volley and the guerrillas took no losses. Usually when the fighting started, Sitoy was under strict orders to keep his head down and not move until ordered to do so by the patrol leader or by his *Manong*, the older brother assigned to watch him. The concern for Sitoy had become more than affection; his skill as a medic made him too valuable to lose.

As the guerrillas examined the bodies and rummaged through the butchery, they seemed to Sitoy to have become much less hurried and even casual, almost like shoppers in an open-air market. Perhaps the years had seasoned them, creating a confidence that bordered on arrogance. It was early 1944, and even though MacArthur had not yet returned, everyone knew he would do so soon. Their attitude now was much as Sitoy's had been during an earlier time, before the Japanese came.

From under the shade of a large, overhanging rock, Sitoy watched as the other guerrillas gathered around the dying Korean. He knew a decision was being made—the Korean would pay in pain far greater than he now endured. The war was like that now for Filipinos, more for revenge than defense. That was fine with Sitoy.

Long ago, Sitoy recalled, he had patiently waited to trap

Joselito, an older childhood rival and the source of considerable torment. Joselito had gone beyond the unspoken boundaries of their continuing competition. He had wrestled Sitoy to the ground and, rather than stop, had brutally pummeled him, blackening both eyes and breaking his nose. For two months, Sitoy brooded and plotted his revenge. His brother Gabriel would be returning from his studies in Cebu City. Although "Gabby" was five years older than Sitoy, he wasn't much bigger. But he was muscular, as many peasant boys are, in a wiry sort of way and he had, during his childhood scuffles, shown a certain talent with his fists. Joselito left Sitoy alone when Gabby was around.

"Strong, fast, clever," nodded Manoling Durano, their neighbor, and old Manoling should have known. In the 1920s he had boxed professionally in Cebu City and Manila as "Kid Moro," although the sobriquet was wholly deceptive, since Manoling was neither young then nor a Muslim. Still, he had had a good career and was once even invited to fight in New York.

"In de Garden," he repeatedly reminded Sitoy and Gabby, in broken English learned from an American constabulary officer who was also a fight fan.

Manoling turned the Garden invitation down, preferring to remain, as some did, the "biggest fish in dis small pond." But Gabriel, according to Manoling, would be different. He'd see that Gabby, when he was in Cebu, would also have a good trainer—"da bery best,'" he assured—and would sharpen his skills at the Cebu Coliseum, which was then the main hippodrome for pugilism in all of Asia, outside of Manila.

Gabby's boxing career progressed rapidly during his stay in Cebu. Fighting three-round bouts as an amateur, he moved quickly up the ladder, winning fights of local, then regional, and finally national import. The next step—signing a professional contract and fighting in the U.S.—was all but assumed by everyone but Gabby. Then one day, as he had indicated in a letter to Sitoy and their parents, he returned to the village. Sitoy, who recognized his brother from a distance of 400 meters, was the first to greet him. He ran what must have been record time for a twelve-year-old. His mind was bursting with stories to tell—like last night, when he had cracked an unsuspecting Joselito with a heavy rattan cane, first in the knee then in the forehead, knocking him cold—but the telling could wait. He just wanted to hug the brother he loved and admired, whose return made sweet vengeance possible.

A month after Gabby's return, the Japanese swept in at dawn from the north. Some shot and sprayed small-arms fire in half arcs, while others lit the thatched roofs of the nearest huts, dooming those who were still inside. That morning, the boys' mother had gone for water at the village pump while their father gathered kindling for the breakfast fire. Both were among the first to fall.

Since the family's hut was at the southern end of the village, there was time to escape. Gabby, as small as he was, grabbed Sitoy and placed him like a rice sack over his shoulder as he ran for the adjoining woods. As Gabby ran, Sitoy, who was still half asleep, started to cry. "The gloves," he whimpered, "the gloves."

The gloves were from Gabby's last fight in Manila, the day he decided he would not turn professional. He had just knocked out the U.S. Army bantamweight champion in stunning fashion—a precise three-punch combination—and the ensuing melee was predictable. Manila's big-time promoters and managers, with visions of peso-to-dollar exchange rates dancing in their heads, crowded the champion-to-be in his dressing room, poking him with pens and pointing to where he should sign. Gabby put them off that day, saying in his simple and calm Cebuano way that such a matter was so important, it was bigger than himself. He'd have to go home to discuss it with his family. Tradition, you know, which he hoped they would understand.

Gabby, of course, did not intend to continue fighting. As he explained one day to Sitoy, it was simply because he was educated and could do something other than box.

"I love school," he explained, "but I also love boxing. But you know, the great Filipinos—Garcia, Villa, Santos—they fight in the States and don' never come back. It was a tough choice, mebbe my toughest, but. . . this is where I stay, 'specially now when times are tense and mebbe there's war."

Gabby then reached into his sack and handed Sitoy a gift, from the younger brother's perspective, a treasure of stunning and precious beauty: a worn pair of brown, American-made, ten-ounce gloves.

"For you," Gabby said quietly. "They're from my last fight, but all that's over now."

Funny things are done under pressure. Gabby put Sitoy face down among a cluster of rocks, tall and wide enough to hide his brother. "Stay down, and don't move" he warned him. Then he turned to run toward home, promising to return with the gloves.

Sitoy was safe, at least for the moment, hidden maybe a hundred meters beyond the southern edge of the village. Gabby figured a moment was all he would need before he returned to continue their flight.

Sitoy lay perfectly still, the side of his face pressed to the ground. He did not move even after an hour had passed, and then another, until finally the sun had found its mid-morning niche. He didn't move even when he heard a nearby "ping"— an ominous and unfamiliar noise—and felt a deep burn in the front of his neck. He knew then that something was terribly wrong. His eyes grew unfocused, darkness gradually replaced light, but still he tried not to move, because Gabby had told him not to and Sitoy loved him so very much.

At the Canebrake

For Sitoy, the discussion about the Korean seemed intolerably long. It was too much. From the sun's position, it was near midday. He felt his eyes start to close. The voices of the others, once clear, now jumbled, started to fade even more. In their place he heard, or thought he did, the distant staccato of small-arms fire. It was Mandaue once more, and the gunfire meant that Japanese reinforcements were on their way.

At Mandaue, he was crouching in a canebrake next to a road now littered with Japanese dead. With him were Aniceto and Poncing, two young but seasoned guerilla veterans whose task it was to provide cover for the main group's withdrawal into the canebrake. As the rest disappeared into the safety of the brake, Sitoy continued to crouch on one knee. He was watching his two comrades pour fire on an enemy yet unseen.

Suddenly, Aniceto fell, pitching forward face first. Instinctively, Sitoy knew he was dead even before he hit the ground—an impression confirmed by the blood that soon stained the back of his head. From his position, Sitoy could see Aniceto's Thompson machine gun, its uselessness endangering not just Poncing and him, but the rest of their group as well. Sitoy jumped out and ran toward the Thompson. The Japanese had not yet noticed him and were concentrating their fire on Poncing, who was thirty meters away on Sitoy's left, pinned behind the stump of an old mango tree.

Poncing's situation was desperate, and Sitoy could see that his religious comrade was preparing to die. Even as Poncing fired, his white rosary beads were out of his pocket and resting uneasily on his thigh.

"Poncing!" Sitoy wanted to shout. "There's no time for that! Older brother, we're not dead yet!" Instead he fired a shot over Poncing's head, rousing him from premature thoughts of the afterlife. Poncing immediately looked up, and was both surprised and embarrassed by a reprieve from such an unlikely source.

"Dear sweet Jesus," Poncing murmured happily. "A child shall lead."

As the Japanese turned their guns toward the new threat, Poncing rose slowly in a crouch firing as he backed toward the canebrake. Sitoy did likewise, and as he sprayed the area beyond the road, he could now see his pursuers, two of whom fell from bullets he knew to be his. Although the situation was far too maddening, Sitoy felt a strange somewhat detached elation at the sight of the falling soldiers. He knew he was a soldier now, and his *utang*, from this point on, could be fully repaid. But it was more than that; mixed in with the fear and elation was also a powerful and disturbing urge to go forward and inspect his handiwork.

He fought it then, but the morbid fascination would linger beyond the day, even as he fired his last round before disappearing into the canebrake.

Red Clay

Sitoy was wakened by a shake of his shoulder. Instinctively he rose and followed a man who beckoned him to join the group still gathered around the Korean. As Sitoy approached, the other guerillas parted slightly, allowing him a clear view of the wounded man. Sitoy was surprised he was still alive.

Even had the dying man been a Filipino, Sitoy wouldn't have treated him. The wounds were too severe and the loss of blood too substantial to merit either attention or precious medical supplies. He wondered when the man would finally surrender and marveled at his ability to hang on.

Transfixed, Sitoy watched the soldier's shattered, bloody chest rising and falling in what he knew was a futile struggle. The man was conscious but he made no sound beyond his pounding gasps for air—no cry for help, no acknowledgment of pain. Sitoy listened and watched, as did the others, because that's all there was. This tiny piece of road had become a temporary stage for a dying man's last show. One of the older guerrillas stepped forward, pistol in hand, to put an end to the man's suffering. But he was stopped by the same commanding voice that had earlier stopped Sitoy.

The voice then ordered Sitoy to come forward. *"Marika, bata,"* it said, and dutifully he did.

"Bandage up this Korean," was the next command, this time given in English. And although Sitoy was puzzled by the order and did not understand its reason, he had learned long ago that when Clara Natividad gave orders, the wisest course was to obey.

Sitoy patched what he could. It was the first time he had bandaged an enemy soldier and, despite his hatred, he managed to do a creditable job. As he dressed the gaping thigh wound, the Korean inadvertently moaned. Sitoy, moved more by habit than kindness or consideration, instinctively reached for his small medicine kit.

"No morphine," Clara said sharply before Sitoy could pull out the precious pain killer. "That's enough, Sitoy. Just carry him and follow me."

Aided by two others, Sitoy carried the dying Korean and followed Clara. As she led the way, they eventually left the road, passing through woods and finally reaching the level clearing where bones of the unburied rested uneasily atop a ground of reddish hue.

Bathed in sweat, Sitoy and his companions, Carlito and Jose, dropped their heavy human cargo, propping his back against a boulder at the edge of the clearing.

The Korean, though wracked with pain and barely conscious, slowly came to recognize their destination.

"No," he said weakly in English as realization set in. "No!"

"He's the one," Clara said as the other guerrillas gathered around her.

"He's the one," she repeated calmly, looking first at Sitoy, then the other two for any sign of dissent. There was none.

"The baby in the village," she said coldly. "He's the one."

The Korean looked with terror as Clara knelt directly in front of him with a bolo in her right hand, its glint shining through the shade, temporarily blinding him. But he saw the knife flash downward toward his left hand, which rested for support on an adjoining rock.

His scream—deep, black, and primal—froze the blood of the others, rendering Sitoy motionless, unable to walk, his kneecaps suddenly gone. Jose fainted. Carlito doubled over, vomiting as if he might purge himself of the horror of the moment. Only Clara was unmoved.

"Patch him, Sitoy," she said calmly as she wiped the bloody knife on her pant leg.

"Murderer," she spat at the one-handed Korean. "The day's long, and there's more to come."

Hours later, Clara and Sitoy emerged from the woods, their clothes covered with grisly evidence of their work.

Sitoy thought of the Korean and how the others—Jose and Carlito—hid their eyes or fainted as the prisoner died his slow, unnatural death. They soon begged to leave, and Clara dismissed them.

Sitoy almost fainted as well, but Clara told him not to. She depended on him, she said, and that was enough to keep him patching new wounds as Clara continued.

The Korean took hours to die, and beyond the gore and the screams of the dying, Sitoy understood that Clara trusted him to do his work. This he did. In this war without rules, he knew it was another turning point for him as a soldier, like the ambush at Mandaue. The thought pleased him and he smiled; only as a soldier could his *utang* be repaid.

PART III

— 5 —

Dawn:
Good Friday

Deep in the forest, Carlito stopped suddenly at a clearing and disappeared behind a thick clump of underbrush and trees. Loloy, the older of his two companions, slumped to the ground and, with great effort, leaned his back against a tree. He started coughing a vile, old man's tubercular cough. Turning quickly to one side, he spat a noxious wad of phlegm while reaching to his shirt pocket for a cigarette, a habit which Cacoy warned would eventually kill him. No matter, Loloy thought, you die anyway.

Loloy then lit the match and instinctively cupped his hands to protect the precious flame against a nonexistent breeze.

"Marlboro," he sighed happily anticipating the first drag. Philippine cigarettes were OK, but U.S. brands, like U.S. anything, were better.

"Loloy," Cacoy scolded sharply in Cebuano, "you know you shouldn't."

The voice startled Loloy, who looked up, then down, at the tiny flame that was now going out.

"Damn!" he muttered, as he reached for another match, his last. He struck again, waiting for the flame to stabilize before drawing it to him. It met the same fate as its predecessor. In frustration, Loloy flung the Marlboro to the ground.

"Time to quit anyway," he said without much conviction to Cacoy, who tried not to smile. The smile came anyway, and gradually Loloy's resolve to be miserable disappeared.

"Hell," Loloy said as he picked up the Marlboro and put it back in his shirt pocket. "I lied. And besides, it's a sin to waste."

On occasional moments, sweet and wordless, a joke is shared and mirth is caught in another's eye. Yet, in that clearing, the warmth of the moment flickered out in a growing and troubling realization—that the silence was unnatural, pervasive, undisturbed by other sounds. Worse, the man who had brought them to this soundless, windless place on the far edge of the woods was now gone, nowhere to be seen.

Loloy rose slowly to his feet, eyes darting fearfully side to side like marbles in a bell jar. Once standing, he reached to touch Cacoy, who moved even closer to his friend. Loloy, because of his age, should have taken control. But he didn't. It was left to the younger man to underscore what, in the folds of their hearts, both felt but couldn't say.

"There!" Cacoy raised his bony arm covered by a tattered cotton sleeve, too long for what it covered. From the cuff emerged a thin, mud-brown finger, shaking like a snake on a leash. To Loloy, who was by now thoroughly spooked, the finger seemed almost to have a life of its own.

"There," Cacoy said again, but more firmly and under better control. "That's where we came from, and hope to God leave that way too."

Cacoy moved first. He walked silently, like a father leaving a sleeping baby's crib, and he heard Loloy's footsteps fall in quietly behind him. Cacoy was tempted to look back at that odd and eerie clearing, with its curious red clay surface that had stained the back of Loloy's clothes. But he recalled vaguely the admonition given Lot's wife. He resolved, at least for the moment, to look straight ahead.

After maybe twenty minutes, the pace behind Cacoy, at first easy and cadenced like a metronome on a piano top, had become uneven. Then came a gurgle and a gasp for breath, followed by footsteps that fell much slower, and, finally, not at all.

"Goddam cigarettes!" Cacoy heard and was comforted by the normality of the tone and sentiment expressed. He also figured they were now far enough from the clearing that the warning to Lot's wife no longer applied. So without fear, he turned to lend assistance to his friend, expecting him to be, as he usually was, bent over and trying to draw breath through his one good lung.

Loloy was there as envisioned, but so too was Carlito, who stood by Loloy's side, talking softly to him and stroking him gently on his back.

Cacoy gasped, unable to contain either his fear or surprise. Carlito took no notice or, if he did, disguised it well. Cacoy simply stared at the old man, whose eyes, though out of focus, were calm and without rancor or any hint of irritation.

Was he possessed? And if so, were they next? And what of Loloy, bent like a rusty coil, wondering from where his next gulp of air would come? No problem there, Cacoy decided. In fact, he was to be envied, preoccupied as he was.

Cacoy had seen that look before—once when he was very young—and he had hoped never to see it again. He recalled it as a combination of righteousness and resignation, and they all had it, those men and women in a small barrio outside the town of Catbalogan, Samar, on the night they buried a young woman alive.

They prayed the rosary on that night as they roped her like a pig for slaughter, claiming she was an adulteress and thus deserving of her fate before God's laws. (Which God they didn't say.) One of her accusers, a young pregnant girl no older than sixteen, tied a small crucifix to the prisoner's belly before the others lowered her into a shallow hole dug in the tide flats.

"Repent," the accuser wailed as her small, pretty features took on a tortured, demonic mien. "Repent."

That night was enough for Cacoy, who resolved then to leave the island of Samar forever. He was only too familiar with Samar's grinding poverty, owing mainly to its position in the middle of the Philippines' typhoon belt. That much he could tolerate. It was everything else about these people on the brink—particularly their chronic despair and its consequence, an arbitrary and cruel superstition passing for faith—that drove him from home. To Cebu, where Chinese banks and money, a mild climate, and a prosperous population promised a different life.

The three walked back toward the clearing. When they finally arrived, it was starting to get dark. Loloy hadn't bargained for this; his stomach, uneasy to start with, began to knot as Carlito disappeared behind a boulder on the edge of the ruddy clearing. He emerged with a sack of tools and two sturdy wooden planks. The longer of the two bore an unusual projection, like a small tabletop, which tilted slightly downward. He handed Cacoy a small hand shovel and commanded him to start digging a narrow hole on a ledge near the far edge of the clearing; from this point the entire valley could be viewed.

Carlito then set the shorter plank across its mate, hammering it into place at a point roughly five feet above the tilted projection. Carlito finished quickly and looked impatiently at Cacoy, wordlessly urging him to finish his task. Dutifully, he quickened his pace. Done, he then dropped the shovel and walked to Carlito, awaiting his next command.

Carlito rose from his crouch and disappeared once more behind the boulder from which he had earlier brought both tools and planks. Loloy, seeing his opportunity, leaped upon his friend.

"Are you crazy? Are you crazy?" Loloy kept repeating the question in a loud and frantic whisper, but Cacoy just stared impassively at him.

"No." Cacoy said.

Moments later, Carlito reappeared with several lengths of rope which he lay on the ground near one end of the crossbeam. He motioned, and Cacoy obediently approached him; he then whispered something Loloy was unable to hear.

"We stay here tonight; then first thing tomorrow we tie him up." Cacoy said flatly to his friend.

"What?"

"We nail him like Jesus on Good Friday. Tomorrow's Good Friday. For tonight he just wants it all ready. He's going away now to think."

"Like Jesus?"

"Yes. Like Jesus. Except he wants to die at dawn."

Early the next morning, ropes bound Carlito's arms tightly to the crossbeam, followed by nails piercing the tarsals of the right hand, then the left. Carlito screamed and bit through his lower lip, oblivious to the blood that quickly covered his chin.

Loloy cringed and hesitated.

"Keep working; keep working," his friend urged.

Next were the feet. The legs had also been tied to wood at thigh and ankle level, with the feet placed one atop the other. The hammer fell twice, and the long, ten-inch nail found its mark, fastening flesh to the small wooden abutment.

Carlito closed his eyes. He didn't feel the unsteady movement of the cross as it was pulled and pushed into place. The pain was so intense; much more than he expected. His only comfort was that soon it would end, and his pact—his negotiation with God—would be sealed. He had seen or heard about others like him who had clutched the cross as their last resort.

But they were different, and he didn't want to be like them. For the others, there was suffering but no death. They'd come down carrying their stigmata like relics for the pious, inspiring devotion among the superstitious so inclined in the first place. Carlito would stay, and as he hung there, he grew prouder of the difference.

He believed he was being punished for an impure life and that his granddaughter's fate was a sign of God's displeasure. A life for a life, Carlito thought. Surely God, Who created the Chinese and blessed their business acumen, could accept this deal. It made sense.

A sudden doubt—he dimly recalled that the Church forbade suicide. For those who chose this godlike and arrogant act, the gates would forever be closed. The thought leaped into clarity, frightening him and displacing momentarily the pain that caused him to twist and writhe.

Too late, he wished he had thought the matter through more clearly. That was just it, he thought. It's too late.

"A life for a life," he mumbled, "and now it will end."

"Cacoy," he gasped. "The spear!"

He would die by piercing, just as Jesus had died. The spear was a small knife with a four-inch blade fastened to the end of a short bamboo cane. Carlito wanted to die quickly. He had made Cacoy promise to kill him upon signal.

"Cacoy, the spear!" he said again.

But, just as the first time, there was no response. Out of the corner of his eye, he saw the makeshift spear, lying useless on the ground. Frantic, he turned his head as best he could, but Cacoy and Loloy were gone. The old man felt a new sensation, far more terrible than pain.

Carlito knew that death would not come for hours, or perhaps days.

—6—

Rumors

In the Philippines, cities spring like warts on smooth skin, aberrations in a land where forests, farmlands, and villages jealously guard their primacy. Even for most city dwellers—refugees from the heartland and a way of life that can feed them no more—the old ways stay etched in their minds and memories. In Cebu they drive cabs, sweep streets, and cook meals for the rich. But among themselves, they speak endlessly about things that matter only to them, to which others, even the rich with their money, are not privy.

On this Monday morning following Jesus's resurrection, when workers were returning to their daily routines after hometown vacations in the countryside, the riders on the jeepney to Mango Avenue talked only of one thing.

"A crucifixion," said Boyet, an old man with stubble on the chin of his dark face. "I heard about it Sunday on the boat back from Negros. When I got to Toledo, my cousin, who's the mayor, said he'd talked to an eyewitness but couldn't remember his name."

"I heard the same thing," added another. "But I thought there were three, like Jesus and the thieves."

"No," the old man said firmly. "Cebu's not that extreme, not like Samar."

"I like Easter," said Estella happily. She was a middle-aged woman who worked for an American couple in Beverly Hills, Cebu's most exclusive district. The wife was extremely religious. Homesick and depressed, she sought comfort in her faith and had brought from the States a huge video collection of biblical epics. Estella, when she had free time, watched them over and over again.

"It's like the movies, you know, like *Ben Hur.* There's this scene..."

"Well, what about this Jesus?" a young man interrupted. He worked in a small bake shop and his stop was next. Like everyone else on the jeepney that morning, he wanted to know, "Has he come down?"

"No," Boyet said with feigned gravity. "As far as I know, he's still there, you know, kind of hanging around." The source of bad humor is its own best audience. As Boyet howled, he was joined by others, mostly out of embarrassment.

"Hanging around, hanging around," he repeated, as a sharp rap on the roof signaled the next stop.

The baker squirmed quickly through the narrow aisle toward the exit. "Then Jesus got problems," he turned and said before stepping off. The notion of Jesus having problems struck the old man as funny and he started to laugh again, this time louder but alone.

One rider who didn't share the mirth that morning was Marites, a slender young *provinciana* from the southern island of Mindanao. The talk of crucifixion bothered her. She was grateful her stop was next.

Mango Avenue. A shaded, walled boulevard that had seen better times. As she walked toward her destination, a fine old stucco house, she was immersed in thought, stopping only once to drop twenty-five centavos in the cup of the legless leper perched on a small wooden platform with wheels. Every morning, he begged at the gate of the stucco house.

"*Daghan salamat*, Marites," he said cheerfully.

Marites was kind. She had given before and the beggar knew her name. But this morning was different. Instead of stopping a moment to chat, as was her fashion, she walked on, shoulders hunched, down the driveway toward the house. The leper, who knew more about sorrow than almost anyone in Cebu, was saddened that a girl so young and good should carry a burden so heavy. With the stump of his rotted right hand, he made a quick sign of the cross, summoning a God he addressed only in epitaphs. He whispered a prayer, not for himself but for her, that somehow the cloud would be lifted.

As Marites pushed open the side door to the kitchen, she welcomed the prospect of her daily routine. The house was staffed by two older maids and a cook who lived in the servants' quarters in a small, adjoining building. Not only was Marites the youngest but she was also the only one living off the compound grounds with her uncle and his family.

In the 1950s, Marites's parents, who had little to lose, migrated to the south, to Mindanao, lured there by the promise of rich, cheap land. Her father cleared a small tract near Cagayan, far from the memory of war, but too far, Marites thought as she was growing up, from everything else as well. Since the age of twelve, her sole obsession was to leave that valley and Mindanao, perhaps for the U.S. or Manila, the latter the fabled venue of the different dramas portrayed in Tagalog comics and movies.

Five years ago, when she was thirteen, she first told her

mother of her dream and was met in return by a riveting look of sadness and betrayal. Her father was more direct: a slap across her face followed by a bamboo rod against the back of her bare, brown legs.

Traces of the beating remained, faintly mottling her even brown skin, but so too did her resolve to leave. One morning, six months past, she simply left, taking time only to advise her mother in perfunctory fashion that she was Manila-bound. Her mother tried to protest, but weakly. She was pregnant again, the second in five years and the eighth overall, and Marites's departure meant one less mouth for the small farm to feed.

Although her mother carried the same look as before, the gaze was far less intense. She reached for a small black wooden box and fumbled for something inside which she thrust at her daughter.

"No Manila," her mother said, pleading. "At least not first. The city will eat you. Cebu first, OK? We have relatives." Her mother grabbed her daughter's hand, placing in it an old white envelope which Marites slipped into her straw handbag.

Marites hugged her mother tightly, careful not to look at her swollen, tearful eyes; then she turned quickly and left. As she walked down the short stairway of the house toward the nearby road, she could hear her father behind her urging the old caribou to pull the plow just a bit harder. She could also see the bus that would start her journey—it was rapidly filling—and she quickened her pace as the back of her legs started to hurt.

Later, on the boat, Marites opened the envelope and saw a thousand-peso bill—less than a hundred dollars U.S., but still more than she'd ever seen in her life—and the names and addresses of relatives in Cebu.

She arrived in Cebu two days later on a pitch-black night,

the city's main generator having broken down two hours earlier. Marites summoned all of her courage, walked away from the dock, and hailed a cab. Silently, she handed the driver the list of relatives written in her mother's hand. Nervously, she pointed with her finger at the place to stop.

"Mango?" he asked

She nodded.

Through narrow streets the cab skidded and wound, missing pedestrians, animals, and other cars by what seemed to her to be fractions of inches.

As the cab halted abruptly in front of a tall iron gate, Marites searched in her handbag, clutching the precious bill with her right hand while groping for change with the other. There was little, and she was certain there wasn't enough for the fare. She sat back perplexed.

The driver sensed her confusion. Shaking his head he said, *"Libre, Inday."* And because he wasn't sure just where she was from, he spoke again, in English rather than Cebuano. "I'm from the country myself. Next time, OK?"

Relieved and thankful, Marites got out of the car and rang the bell on the gate. She whispered who she was to the old man who came forward to answer. He scratched his head and beckoned her to enter. As she turned toward the house, Marites could see the cab's lights against the white stucco wall move quickly and then disappear as the cabbie, his deed of mercy completed, drove loudly into the night.

Marites and the servant were greeted at the door by a tall older woman. Her black hair, straight and unadorned, fell to the nape of her neck. She was barefoot and wore a long robe. Marites guessed her to be over fifty and, although the light provided by a solitary candle in the front window was dim, she struck the girl as being extremely beautiful.

Marites reached for the woman's hand, intending to press it

to her own forehead while simultaneously mumbling her introduction. She accomplished the latter, but the hand was gone. Instead, Marites found herself pulled forcefully forward and then smothered in a strong embrace.

"So you're Josefa's daughter!" the woman said loudly as she rocked the girl from side to said. Poor Marites tried to respond, but she was pinned too firmly even to nod her head.

"Of course I'll help," the woman said repeatedly, "but on one condition. From now on call me Tia. Tia Clara."

Marites's six months in Cebu had been more than she could ever have imagined. The pay was good, so much so that she had managed to save her thousand-peso bill, and her duties, what duties there were, were light. (She assisted the maids, who were ordered by Clara not to work her too hard.)

Marites was even offered a room in the house itself, away from servants' quarters. But the girl declined, protesting that she had already imposed too much.

Marites soon discovered other evidence that she had chosen her patron well. Her aunt was rich and powerful, and the house in Cebu was but one of several Clara owned in the Philippines. Tia Clara spent most of her time in Manila, but she visited Cebu often. To Marites, Clara's life seemed perpetually in transit.

This past Easter Week, however, had been different. Clara had stayed in Cebu, hosting Ben Lucero, a young priest from Seattle who was in the Philippines for the first time. He had arrived in Cebu two weeks earlier to bury his Philippine-born mother. Every effort was being made to ease his burden, a burden Clara shared.

On that morning, as Marites started her usual round of chores—preparing and serving coffee to Clara and a diverse, changing ménage of house guests—she could see her aunt and the priest sitting silently in the dining room. Ben sorted through the five or six local and national newspapers to which Clara subscribed, while Clara, cigarette in hand, looked away, hiding her thoughts behind lines of thin, white smoke.

Their sorrow unnerved Marites; she had never seen her aunt so. Sorrow had begun to seem tangible and real since the coming of the priest, seeping like moisture into the pores of each wall. And this morning was no different. In her young life, she had seen the dead, many of them, embalmed and presented for relatives to photograph. But she had never lost someone close. Was there someone close? She wondered. Marites had never mourned and her heart was still whole. She wondered also about sorrow, if she'd feel it, or even if she could.

The doubts bothered her, adding to earlier concerns as she readied the tray for service. She soon finished her task and, laden with mangoes and coffee, entered the next room.

"Good morning," Marites said in English, in deference to the guest.

Her voice seemed to jolt them both, forcing a faint smile of recognition from Ben, and from Clara, a greeting in return.

"Good morning, dear," Clara said quietly.

"The mangoes are fresh, Tia," Marites advised, "and in the kitchen there's also... "

Never mind, Marites," Clara interrupted with a wave of her hand, "this is enough, unless Ben... "

The priest shook his head as he mixed his coffee with thick brown sugar and enough cream to turn it white. Both seemed to welcome this first meal and the break in reverie it provided.

"Come here," Clara commanded Marites, "and tell your auntie about your holiday."

On ordinary days, Marites welcomed Clara's attention. Her

aunt was solicitous and maternal, particularly after she'd return from days or even weeks of absence. Marites thought it was because Clara had no children, or, if she did, she'd never seen them around this house. It was such a change from Cagayan, the young girl often thought, where life's hardships made conversations short. Her openness with her aunt always surprised her; she would tell Clara everything, losing time and a bit of herself as well. Through it all, Clara would sit and nod, blowing smoke out of both nostrils—sometimes just one, for the girl's amusement—and would say little.

Marites was especially touched by the grieving woman's concern. But today wasn't an ordinary day, and she didn't know where to begin. The two women sat close together, much closer than ever before. And Marites leaned over to speak in a voice just above a whisper.

"Tia, I'm afraid."

"Of what?"

"Nothing," Marites said slowly. "I mean, not for me—for Lolo Carlito. You know Lolo Carlito. He says he knew you before the war. He's the best friend of my Tio Loloy. He's always over at the house, and he's a good, kind man. But you know, for the last two months he's been so sad. Once he even said he'd kill himself. But, of course, I didn't believe him."

"You shouldn't," Clara said calmly. "I know Carlito. He used to work here for me, but I had to fire him. Do you know why? He was always drunk, and when he was sober. . . never mind. Nothing's happened to Carlito that maybe a few days spent drying up won't help."

"But Tia, I haven't seen either of them for most of Easter Week, and all that time, Tia Masay—that's Loloy's wife—well, we were worried. Then I saw my uncle late last night, and when I asked him about Lolo Carlito, he just turned away."

"So?"

"So, I heard Lolo talking to my uncle last Easter Monday. He wanted him to come with him to this place by the Toledo Road. I know he drinks, but this time he was sober, and when they saw me, they just got real quiet."

"What place?"

"Just a place in the woods. That's all I heard—that, and something about red dirt."

"Red what?"

"I'm not sure. It's just a place in the woods by the Toledo Road. And then this morning, on the way over here, I heard about this crucifixion."

"A what?" The priest entered the conversation for the first time.

"Nothing, Ben," Clara said, her tone dismissing the topic. "It's just every Easter, some religious fanatics have themselves stapled to the cross.

Ben's curiosity slowly gave way to anger. "That's not Catholicism. What about the bishop?"

"Bishops live in palaces," Clara said sternly, "or at least in places better than most. You should know that, too. And besides, everybody's happy after it's over. Those fools come down and show their wounds. Stupid people honor them and ask for their intercession. Everyone's piety is increased, and the bishop's happy. Everybody's happy."

Clara paused, knowing that her cynicism had an effect. She relished for a heartbeat the discomfort of her audience.

"But Tia," Marites said quietly, "that's just it. This time he didn't come down."

It was just past ten and the city's streets were already clogged. Dust and exhaust fumes swirled and danced with the slow movement of traffic, blending above it all with smoke from trash burned in open spaces. In the narrow VW van, Ben sat cramped and erect between Clara and Marites. Seated in front, next to the driver, was Loloy, silent and sullen.

After Marites had told her tale, Clara and Ben had accompanied her to her uncle's house.

"Take us, Tio," Marites pleaded.

Loloy turned sharply away, fearful, denying at first that he knew what his niece spoke of, then pleading his innocence.

"Take us," Marites repeated.

Loloy retreated farther into the house, his eyes darting like waterbugs. He hoped the others wouldn't follow, but they did, led by Clara.

"You know, Loloy," Clara said flatly. "Murder's a serious crime, and my nephew Alonzo is the assistant to the police chief. . . . "

As the van crossed the southern edge of the city, congestion lessened. There were rice fields on both sides of the road, and farmers, stooping and knee-deep in mud, never looking up. The changed scene seemed to release some of the tension in the van. Ben, whose American sense of order was offended by Cebu's chaos and pollution, slouched forward. He was now in a more amiable mood, striking up a conversation in badly mangled Cebuano with Rey, the driver.

Rey was tolerant and Clara amused. As she listed, she figured the ratio at about ten English words to one Cebuano. But at least Ben tried, which was more than could be said for most Americans.

They were about twenty minutes outside the city, and by then Ben had learned fifteen new words and phrases, all of which were dutifully scrawled into his notebook. Marites had also joined in the process of educating the American. Their chatter—lively but meaningless—was a temporary block on the macabre.

Clara was pleased but silent, occupied by other thoughts. The van turned right onto the narrow dirt trail which marked the start of the road to Toledo. As it slowly climbed past trees and huts, she recognized a stream to her left—free-flowing but brown from human waste and debris. It hadn't always been that way. Almost forty years ago, the people were fewer and the trees surrounding the stream far thicker, enough, at least, to give a wounded and frightened girl shelter for a moment.

She remembered the white boulder, oblong and smooth, where she lay on her back, her shoulder shredded with what she didn't know. It was her first wound, but she had to clean it somehow and cover it as best she could.

Drained of strength, she lay on her back on the boulder that touched the edge of this hidden, pristine stream. With her good right arm, she reached for the water, tilting her head backward. To steady herself she grabbed—or tried to—a small protrusion in the boulder's otherwise smooth surface. The problem was that what she had seen and knew to be there, she couldn't feel, much less hold. The fingers on her bad hand, stiff and clawlike, bounced like a rake on a rough cement floor. She could feel herself sliding backward, head first, into a cold pool of water. But there wasn't much she could do.

"Shit," she thought, as the back of her head hit the stream bottom. "So this is it."

Clara's blood colored the water, clouding her sight, red giving way to final black. Then a confusion of dark brown and white took shape—the round face of Sitoy, smiling and mute, not more than six unfocused inches from her own. Sitoy had bandaged her and brought her a bowl of broth. She could make out the inside of a tent and could hear traces of familiar voices. Clara guessed she was back in camp in the hills above Cebu.

"Sorry, *Inday*," said a voice from the entrance. "We had to leave you. There were too many. Good thing Sitoy went back."

Sitoy, the designated doctor, was as fussy as a new mother. Since he couldn't talk, he motioned with a bowl and spoon, mouthing the Cebuano command to eat. Clara wasn't hungry and she certainly was in no mood to be spoon-fed, whatever her condition. Her lack of interest only prodded Sitoy, making him more aggressive as he moved bowl, spoon, and his face ever closer to Clara.

"*Kaon.*" Sitoy breathed.

Weak as she was, Clara managed to push the palm of her good hand on Sitoy's advancing nose, straightening her arm and locking the elbow.

"Your breath, Sitoy," she whispered before losing consciousness once more.

Your breath, Sitoy," Clara murmured.

"Pardon, Ma'm?"

"Nothing, Rey."

As the van moved up the mountain, gaining altitude and relief from flatland heat, Clara opened her window.

"Turn off the air-con, Rey. It's cool here," Clara said.

Like a rambunctious schoolgirl, Clara then stuck her head out the window savoring the breeze, sweet and clean. It was a treat unknown to those living below. She'd almost forgotten that, during the Occupation, the wind would touch her face and neck almost like a lover; it was one of her few pleasures in a routine of boredom and terror. At the end, Clara walked away from the hills and four years of her life, thinking never to return, hoping not to remember.

The sudden shift of gears signaled journey's end. The road had reached its apex, and from this point, after a short, flat stretch, it would be downhill toward Toledo and the sea. Upon Loloy's signal, Rey pulled the van over and turned off the ignition, the engine humming for a while, then dying. Inside, everyone was quiet and still.

"Come on," Clara finally said. "We'll follow Tio."

Loloy chafed at the prospect and looked hard at Clara. Clara returned the stare, overcoming his intensity with her own.

"Go ahead, Loloy," she commanded.

"Go, goddam you!" she said as she grabbed the back of his hair and pushed him out the door.

Once outside, Loloy shook his head like he was punch-drunk. His dark, brown face flushed and tightened, twisting his plain and placid features into a sudden ominous mask. He ran wildly at Clara as she stepped from the van, pushing her back inside. As he clawed at her neck, Ben rushed in, pulling Loloy from his aunt. The priest used his weight to smother and subdue the smaller man.

Ben lay atop his foe for several minutes, draining the old man of anger and the will to fight. He stood up, then stooped to help Loloy to his feet. As Loloy started to rise, his knees buckled and he suddenly pitched forward, a small, red gash visible on the back of his head.

Behind Loloy stood Rey, a rock the size of his fist still clenched in his right hand. Blood colored part of its gray surface, lightly brushing the tips of his fingers.

On seeing her uncle fall, Marites ran to him. Kneeling at his side, she gently cradled his head in her arms. He eventually came to.

"I'm OK," he said slowly. "I'm OK. Just leave me here."

"But Tio!" she cried. "We'll call this off and take you home. It's my fault, I never should have..."

"Just never mind," he snapped." I'm OK. Just never mind.

"Ask the bitch," Loloy added, pointing at Clara. "She knows where Carlito is. Have *her* take you."

Loloy's gaze, searing and unrepentant, focused on Clara, bringing from her an uncharacteristic response—she blinked and turned briefly away. From the others, silence, broken only by Loloy's hoarse, derisive laughter.

"Go on, Dona Clara, take them," he cackled. "Take them. And tell them, too!"

After a pause, Clara replied. "You heard the old fool," she said calmly. "Just follow me."

Tentatively at first, then more surely, Clara walked through the underbrush. She stopped at different spots, trying to divine a path that had long since vanished which she had long since forgotten. After half an hour—Ben knew because he nervously tracked the time on his watch—she stopped once more.

"There," she said. "It's there, beyond those trees."

"Are you sure?" Ben asked nervously. He was the only one among them with enough standing to question his aunt.

"Yes," she said mildly. "If Carlito's anywhere, he's there."

Despite her assurance, no one moved.

"Well, come on," Clara said impatiently. "We didn't come here for nothing."

Tentatively, Ben stepped forward ahead of his aunt, followed by Marites. Rey remained behind Clara, giving the appearance of motion but no real movement.

Like hunters stalking, they walked single file toward the small stand of trees. They were silent and nervous, as if the dead could hear—if indeed Carlito was dead, or even nearby.

Ben was the first to arrive. He had quickened his pace, distancing himself from Marites and Clara. He felt embarrassed at the morbid excitement—it seemed unpriestly—that pounded in his head. As he reached the clearing, the stench of decomposition hit him first, like the rock that felled Goliath. His initial reaction was to scan the red earth. Nothing there. Raising his eyes, he stared transfixed, stunned. Slowly, he turned and walked back to the others.

"He's there," he whispered, his face without color, as he continued to walk slowly back toward the Toledo Road.

Marites and Clara were next. As they reached the clearing, Ben vaguely heard a scream—maybe they both screamed—then a long train of sobs.

Carlito was here, as Ben had said and Marites had feared. His body was black and limp, and although his feet were secured by rope, his upper torso dangled from his right hand affixed to the crossbeam. His left arm hung free, swaying in fitful motion when the wind started.

Part of his left hand remained on the crossbeam, evidence of his struggle to free himself. Behind the two women, unnoticed by all, Rey stood, three clicks revealing his presence.

Carlito's worst day would be remembered by Polaroid.

PART IV

—7—

The Aftermath

The day after their return from the Toledo Road, the crucifixion haunted Ben. He could see it and even smell it. He was the exception; his companions had returned to normal. Later that morning, Clara went to the police station to notify Alonzo, her nephew. Ben went with her.

Alonzo was in a small office, seated behind an old metal table. He was a big man, bigger than most Filipinos. His face was pock-marked and heavy jowled, and his hair was short, cut in a style Jack Webb would have approved. Embedded in the fleshy folds of his face were a pair of tiny black eyes incapable, Ben thought, of expressing joy.

Earlier, Ben noticed that policemen in Cebu were uniformly large, and it had puzzled him.

"Were they chosen for size?" he had asked Clara.

"Not really," she said. "They're small when they start. But, you know, police work in Cebu has certain privileges."

"Like extortion?"

"Like privileges."

As the three sat in the hot, stuffy office, Alonzo rose quickly and disappeared into an adjoining room, his padded ass so huge it almost followed after—the most evident beneficiary of police privileges.

With Alonzo's sectional exit, Ben whispered maliciously, "Your nephew's never missed a meal."

"Shhh," she hissed. "He's coming back now."

Alonzo reentered, like a dancer on cue, a yellow note pad in his right hand, his left holding a pair of expensive-looking eyeglasses. With great care, he buffed the lenses with his dangling shirt front and put them on. Alonzo was perspiring heavily. By the time he sat down, the smooth, flat bridge of his nose proved insufficient to its task. The glasses slid quickly, their resistible force impeded by an immovable pair of bulbous nostrils. Alonzo seemed not to notice.

As Clara recounted her story, the policeman looked intently at her like an obedient student, taking great care to jot down notes at appropriate points. Clara spoke in Cebuano, and Ben could not understand most of the conversation. Finally the interview was over, and Alonzo, looking grave, promised in English to investigate the matter and send some men to retrieve poor Carlito's remains.

Clara and Ben then left the station and waited for Rey, the driver. Clara smiled. "Alonzo's lazy," she said, "but he'll follow up on this."

"Why?"

"He's my nephew for one, and besides," she said smugly, "I got him the job." Her tone of voice indicated an end to the messy business.

But for Ben it was far from over. Carlito's act was blasphemous, and, in his view, fundamentally antireligious. As they drove back toward Mango Avenue, he struggled to understand what it was within Catholicism, or maybe culture, that drove

Carlito to his death—and worse—Filipinos to accept so blandly his demise.

"You have to understand, nephew," Ben remembered Clara saying to one of his inquiries, "it's a little different around here."

Different, he thought, recalling the conversation as the car neared Mango Avenue. Different. How different?

"Tia," Ben said suddenly as Rey stopped for a crossing horse-drawn calesa, "I think I want to get out here."

"But Ben, we're near home. Have lunch first. It's ready, you know. Then you may go."

"But Tia, I'm not really hungry."

Clara was about to protest, but Ben had already opened the door and was two steps toward the nearest curb. She rolled down the window. "Just call Rey when you need a ride home," Clara shouted.

Ben nodded with indifference as he turned backward to look. Approaching was a jeepney heading for downtown Cebu. He quickened his pace. A line was forming at the corner, and he intended to be aboard.

It was almost noon when Ben stepped off the jeepney. By then, downtown was packed with people and traffic. He had been in Cebu two weeks now, but this was his first time in the city's core. He hated the heat but welcomed the commotion. There was anonymity in the crowded sidewalks—people moving like currents in different directions. It was fine with him; he had no particular destination, and this type of movement, thoughtless and compliant, was perfect for now.

He walked this way, for how long he wasn't sure, past rows of dim shops and loud street vendors, until suddenly the crowds that had propelled him diminished, then disappeared. He looked at his watch—two hours had passed—and he went to a nearby street corner to get his bearings.

The corner was no help. The street sign was up, but the name it once carried had long since faded. Down the block, he heard voices—a lure to the lost. Ben walked toward the sound, rounding the next corner. He saw Rey, his aunt's driver, perhaps halfway down the block in the middle of a small, motley group.

As Rey spoke, some nodded solemnly while others made the sign of the cross. Ben watched and listened; he could understand the Cebuano word for "price," followed by Rey's extended palm, soon covered with multicolored paper money and the glint of silver coins.

Carlito's crucifixion was for sale. Realizing this, Ben backed slowly away. His stomach churned and he ran to a nearby alley. There, forehead and palms pressed against a damp, slimy wall, he tried to vomit, but nothing came forward. The best he got was a growl from his guts and throat.

A few minutes later, he staggered back into the sunlight. He resembled a drunk; his watery, reddish eyes bulged like a Chihuahua's, and saliva glittered at the corners of his mouth. More than anything else, Ben wanted to leave Cebu—tonight if possible. With that foremost in his mind, he hailed a cab to return to Mango Avenue. He'd tell Aunt Clara; she'd make the arrangements. Standby was OK, as long as he knew there was a chance of leaving.

O h Ben," Clara said with disappointment, "you have to understand. Things are a little different. Filipinos take photos of the dead, and I know it's strange to Americans, but it's common here. OK, maybe Rey went too far, but things aren't... "

Clara paused in midsentence and glanced at Ben. His look—so young, forlorn, and American—touched her.

"Never mind," she sighed with a slow shake of her head before resuming her soliloquy. *"Ugma sa buntag*—that means, 'Tomorrow morning's OK.' OK? I'll come with you to Manila, I've got business to take care of. You can book for the States there."

"And besides," Clara said smiling, "I'll have a chance to show you the city."

The trip from Manila International to the heart of the city ordinarily takes twenty-five minutes, but Clara's driver made it in a little more than half the time. The air-conditioned Mercedes screeched and sped along Roxas Boulevard, the broad avenue along Manila Bay. In the back seat, Ben sat nervously with his aunt.

"Sitoy," Clara said pointing to the driver, an old man maybe in his late fifties, "doesn't speak English or anything else. But he'd like to be a stock car driver in the States, right?"

Sitoy nodded.

"But who'll hire him? He's too old and he can't talk—during the war the Japs fixed that—now Manila will have to do." Clara pointed to a small scar, down and toward the right on the back of his neck.

"Where the bullet left," she explained solemnly, then quickly changed the topic.

"Sitoy first saw the racers on your Armed Forces Network. The problem is that he practices on my cars. I'd fire him, but otherwise he's a good boy."

Sitoy, the "boy," smiled and nodded again. He had worked for Clara for more years than he could recall. She was, he knew, capable of many things, some of them harsh, of which firing him wasn't one.

Sitoy saw a clear stretch of road and gunned the car. Instinctively, Ben's right hand clutched the rear armrest as the

Mercedes started to weave in and out of heavy morning traffic. Reluctantly, Sitoy heeded a traffic light, and Ben relaxed momentarily, the color returning to his knuckles.

It was Ben's first time in Manila. Upon arriving in the Philippines, he had simply switched planes at the airport, taking the first domestic jet to Cebu. He turned his focus away from Sitoy to examine both sides of the boulevard. He was stunned by the contrast. In the bay, scores of ships lay anchored, while along its shore, dark, dirty people scurried from under bushes and makeshift shelters. Across Roxas lay another world, a city vibrant and wealthy, with rows of new apartments and hotels, most of which had been recently built.

"Squatters," Clara said pointing to the shore. "Many are from the country, and times are hard there. So they come here and live on the streets. They're not supposed to be here, but they come anyway, and the government's stopped trying to keep them out.

"Over here," Clara said, her eyes shifting across the boulevard, "is evidence of a universal truth. The rich like aesthetics. They like views of the sunset on the bay.

"And," she added, "maybe the poor do, too."

Abruptly, the Mercedes made a sharp left turn toward the bay, stopping in front of an impressive white stucco building with a green tile roof.

"This, Nephew, is the Manila Hotel, and you'll be staying here. Nice, eh?"

Ben looked confused.

"But, Tia," he said, "I thought I'd be at your place overnight then back home tomorrow. That's still the plan, isn't it?"

"That was the plan," she explained, "but U.S.–bound is backed up two weeks, and until then, you'll stay here."

"I can't afford this place," Ben said, but his protest was interrupted by the arrival of a thin, stylishly dressed man who approached Clara's side of the car. She smiled in silent recognition.

"It's taken care of," Clara said firmly. "George is the manager and he'll look after you, and Junior, my other driver, will pick you up at six o'clock for dinner. See you then."

Clara's clipped cadence—so different from her usual rhythm—said to Ben that his aunt had made up her mind. He'd heard her use it in the past, with people whose lives she controlled or influenced, but never with him. Like the others, however, he averted his eyes before realizing the nature of his reaction. By then, he was out the door, a bit flustered and irritated, watching the Mercedes, under Sitoy's reckless hand, speed away.

"The boy will take your bag," a voice said. It belonged to George, who signaled for a valet to come forward. This "boy," Ben guessed, was at least forty, and wore a white Philip Morris–style uniform, complete with braid trim and pillbox cap. Both followed George into the hotel lobby, past other similarly dressed "boys" and their civilian-clad supervisors, all of whom acknowledged the leader of this small parade.

The hotel's interior surprised Ben; it was huge and elegant, all marble floors and mahogany panels, and its denizens were all handsome, the women in particular; they resembled the fair-skinned, straight-nosed models he'd seen back home in old copies of the *Philippines Free Press*.

"Pinays are beautiful, da bes'. No can beat," his father's Filipino buddies used to brag. And for evidence, they'd point to the *Free Press* and its latest bevy of rising stars.

"Benny," they'd say after a couple of beers. "They got long legs, light skin, and Español nose—no can beat."

He was young then and prone to belief, and they were army lifers like his father. Ben might have bought their story but for one contradiction; the traits they praised, they didn't possess.

They were short men with flat noses, and some had skin the color of Mississippi mud. The beauties they bragged about would never have looked twice, and "Benny," as he was then known, wasn't even sure such women existed.

Maybe they were flown in from Europe?

No, no. They were real, the old Filipinos assured him.

"And what's great for you, Benny, is that you can have one, maybe two, easy as pie. You're good-looking, you're tall, and you got U.S. citizenship. Maybe even a Miss Universe, eh? Or at least a Miss Philippines. Home got lots of 'em."

Despite Ben's doubts, the vaunted Pinays gave rise to pleasant, pubescent fantasies—the source of countless, puzzling midnight ejaculations until he was fourteen. All was extinguished then because Remedios, who never forgot her wartime vow, enrolled him in the seminary. There he stayed, outgrowing puberty and sidestepping its attendant problems.

Ben recalled all of this as he strolled the marble lobby. As he walked, he felt a twitch in his groin. His old dream—like a theme from Poe—was buried but not dead.

D o you have a name?" Ben asked the bellman as the elevator door opened to the sixth floor. George had remained in the lobby.

"Erasmo, sir," came the reply.

"Well, Erasmo," Ben said extending his right hand, "my name's Ben."

Erasmo was surprised by the American's friendly and open demeanor. Guests at this hotel weren't usually like that.

"I know, sir." Erasmo placed Ben's luggage carefully on the floor before grasping the outstretched hand.

"My pleasure," Ben said.

Erasmo smiled. "Come on, sir. I'll show you your room."

"Ben."

"Pardon, sir?"

"My name's Ben."

"OK, Ben." Erasmo smiled again.

The bellman opened the door and walked to the window, drawing the drapes to reveal a stunning view of Manila Bay.

"Nice," Ben said as he sat heavily on the edge of the bed. He then leaned back slowly, fingers intertwined behind his head.

"You'll like it here," Erasmo said.

"Seems that way."

"Can I fix you a drink..." Erasmo paused and caught himself... "Ben?"

"Right. Make mine a strong bourbon soda, and fix one for yourself."

"I can't," Erasmo protested. "Not while I'm on duty..."

"Go on, Erasmo," Ben insisted. "George won't mind. He wants to please Aunt Clara. It's OK."

Erasmo nodded and walked over to a fully stocked liquor cabinet.

So this, Ben thought as the drinks were mixed, is how the rich live away from home. Luxury, liquor, and "aesthetics," and his for two weeks. Not bad.

Erasmo brought the drinks and handed one to Ben, who, by then, had propped his back against a finely carved wooden headboard.

"To Auntie," Ben proposed as he raised his glass.

The bellman smiled and nodded, raising his own and joining Ben in swallowing its contents in one semicircular motion.

Ben rose to fix another drink.

"My aunt," Ben said casually. "What do you know about her?"

In all the years Ben had known Clara, a large part of her past had always been hazy, whether by design or accident he wasn't quite sure. She was rich, that much was clear when she visited the States—"well to do" was his mother's understated description. When he'd press further, Remedios would explain that Clara was "good in business" and would elaborate no more. Back in the States, it puzzled him, but being young, he let the matter drop. Now he was in the Philippines for the first time, and her show of wealth and influence, amplified by its exercise on her home ground, was too obvious to ignore. Away from his aunt and braced by bourbon, he felt free to ask.

"Come on," Ben said impatiently, "you heard. How'd she get to be this way?"

"I, uh, must go, sir," Erasmo said, formality returning. He walked toward the door but paused before opening it.

"She's very powerful," Erasmo said still facing the door. "But you're lucky. It's clear you're one of hers."

Ben shrugged, a bit embarrased by the description. Erasmo then quickly turned the doorknob and was gone before Ben could question him further.

"But Erasmo," Ben shouted as he scanned the now empty hallway. "What does she do?"

There was no answer. He waited a few seconds more, then returned to his bed to fix one, then another drink. The bourbon had its inevitable effect, and he quickly tumbled into a deep slumber. Before losing consciousness, however, he thought briefly of donning shorts and sport shirt and, armed with a camera, hiring a cab to explore the city.

He rejected the idea when he envisioned himself as a taller version of a Japanese tourist.

He had decided to hang around, drink the booze, turn up the air-con, and maybe later visit the lobby. Ben felt so unpriestly here, drunk and relaxed like a sailor on leave. He'd been on vacations before—away from his parish and his duties—but the awareness of his vocation had never left him. Ben had always been a priest, on duty or off. It was bankable, but this time in Manila was somehow different.

Maybe it was the superstition passing for religion, or his revulsion toward it, or maybe it was just the alcohol, or all of the above. He couldn't tell. What he did know was that he was losing consciousness, a development confirmed by the uniformity of oncoming darkness as he turned his focus from the ceiling to different sides of the room.

On one side he saw his bag, which contained his white Roman collar, and he remembered vaguely that he had worn it last at his mother's burial. Drunk as he was, he also knew he wouldn't take it out in Manila. It was, he thought in his blurred state, a bit like a puppy in a box; once released, it would jump on him and affix itself to his leg, chest or, in his case, neck. He didn't want that, at least not here.

"Stay," he mumbled at the bag before closing his eyes.

To Ben, the ringing telephone was like the clarion for the Apocalypse. He was lying face down, but he bolted straight up, arching his face and back like a trained seal.

"Shit," he cursed as his body came crashing down. The phone rang again and he reached for it, knocking over half-filled glasses in the process.

"Hello, Ben." The voice was Clara's.

"Oh. Hello, Tia," Ben mumbled.

"It's three o'clock and I'll send Ellen Labrado over to pick you up.

"Who's Ellen Labrado?"

"My assistant. Get ready, OK? She'll be there in a while."

"But Tia. . . " Click. "Shit."

Even in his stupor, Ben could distinguish the imperious edge in Clara's voice. It meant that the mysterious Ellen would be here shortly, and the nephew had best be ready.

But first, there was the matter of the bathroom—its distance—and how best to get there. Should he walk or crawl? Since he was already on his belly, he chose the latter, judging gravity and verticality to be, at the moment, hostile forces. Their attitude toward him would improve, but not before a plunge into a tub of lukewarm water.

As he turned on the tap, Ben grinned. It reminded him of the outstanding feature of fundamentalist baptism—immersion—which he now dearly hoped would heal. It was, he thought, a useful ritual for the drunk and errant.

"Save me, sweet Jesus," he whispered, sliding on his belly like a penguin into water.

H ello, hello. This is Ellen."
The voice was deep, gravelly, and sensuous. To Ben, it was somewhere between Lauren Bacall and the fallen angel. It was also near and quickly getting closer.

Ben had fallen asleep. "Just a second," he said, throwing his tennis shoe hard against the door, closing it somewhat. "I'll be right with you."

He grabbed both edges of the tub and propelled himself upward, finding in the process that gravity was now benign. He reached for a large bath towel, wrapping himself tightly as a nun.

"I'll be right out. Ellen, right? Sorry, I fell asleep."

He reached for the doorknob but was stopped by a bulge between his thighs, creating what looked like a mid-body isosceles triangle, all points and straight lines.

"Shit," he said a bit too loudly, as he unwrapped himself to inspect the culprit, a soapy erection doing a star turn.

"Shit," he said again, grabbing the interloper while thinking of ways to diminish its untimely ardor. He was still a virgin—

dry humping while on vacation from the seminary didn't count—and he'd faced this problem before. But he maintained control and, more important, the appearance of propriety, by thinking of topics that were, by definition, boring.

Economics often worked, particularly macro, the same with Ronald Reagan, as he moved swiftly through his usual litany. But not this time. This was the James Brown of hard-ons, hard-working and not prone to bowing prematurely off the stage. Clearly, something extraordinary was needed.

"American Buddhism," he whispered desperately, and that did the trick, shrinking him like salt does slugs. He quickly rewrapped himself, adopting a mien loaded with propriety.

"I'll be right out," he said.

Ellen sat as she always did when greeting a man—a bit back in the chair, with her long brown legs, bare and tapered, extended and crossed. The hem of her white sundress stopped just above her knees. She was a beautiful young woman, maybe thirty, with finely cut features and dark green eyes.

She looked on with amusement as Ben entered the main room, her beauty prompting an encore from the persistent Mr. Brown. For a brief moment he thought of reinvoking the shibboleth of American Buddhism, but decided against it, thinking it wouldn't work and not sure he'd want it to. Instinctively, he extended his hand, hoping she'd notice this extremity rather than the lower one.

He cut a ludicrous figure. Head back, gut tucked, and arm straight out, he looked like an Oklahoma dowser, divining rod in hand, looking for water.

Ellen tried not to laugh. "Hello, Father," she said innocently. "Your auntie told me everything about you."

The unexpected sound of his religious title was, like American Buddhism, enough to kill his erection.

"Uh, hello," Ben said, a faint blush crossing his face as he weakly shook her hand.

"Excuse me," he quickly added, as he reached for his bag, pulling from it clothes for the evening—a pair of khaki pants and a blue sports shirt. The collar stayed inside. Like a refugee from a bombing, he clutched the clothes to his chest and hurried silently to the bathroom.

"Nice," she purred.

"Pardon me?"

"Nothing."

"Oh."

"I've seen a lot of chests," she added mischievously, "but you're my first priest. Nice."

Ben said nothing as he closed the bathroom door, but under his towel, James skated furiously.

Their next stop was the hotel café. It was a chance for Ben to kill time, sip coffee, and wait for his head and the afternoon traffic to clear.

In that brief span, Ellen said much about herself while Ben mostly listened, a proper and familiar role for a priest. Her father, she was told, was an American (businessman, tourist, soldier, doting parent even for a moment, or one-night stand, she never found out), and the U.S. was her dream. Ben had heard at least the second part many times before. It was like that for millions of Filipinos—an obsession, impossible to discourage, of escape from the province, bound for Manila then San Francisco and beyond. Most didn't make it, but for Ellen he knew the dream was more personal. She was American-made, at least partly, and because she was, she just might succeed.

No, she said, she had never met her father or even seen his picture, but her mother, in one of her few references to him, said he was from Cleveland. He was tall and had green eyes, which explained her own. Ellen's mother, afraid her daughter might leave for the States, refused to say more. When she had died eight years ago, whatever else she knew died with her.

"That old bitch," Ellen said bitterly, referring to her mother. "At least she could have . . . " She cut herself short, remembering that, even without his white collar, the man sitting across from her was a priest.

"I'm sorry, Father," she said contritely.

For a moment, Ben said nothing. He was preoccupied by the woman and her story and surprised by the abrupt end. She had more to say; his instincts as a priest and healer told him that.

Ben's mind scrambled quickly, ultra red alert, its goal a conjunction to a longer train of words, hers not his. He considered something soothing, proper and priestly, like, "It's OK, I understand. Judge not . . . " He was stopped by a voice on the PA.

"Miss Ellen Labrado," it said clearly. "Come to the front, please."

"Ride's here," she said as she rose to leave.

It was almost dark when Junior, Clara's other driver, pulled the Mercedes away from the Manila Hotel.

"Where does Clara live?" Ben asked as he settled into the back seat.

"Forbes," Clara said.

"Forbes?"

"Forbes Park. It's just south of here."

"Sounds cashy."

"Pardon?" Ellen's English was excellent—learned through a steady diet of Hollywood movies—but she hadn't kept up with the vast and shifting realm of American slang.

"Rich."

"It is."

As the Mercedes moved along Roxas, reversing the route taken earlier, Ben enjoyed the last moments of what must have been a magnificent sunset. For an instant, the ragged shoreline and the city beyond were touched by beauty.

"Your first time, isn't it?"

Ben nodded.

"I can tell."

Their small talk, Ben thought, had been exhausted by their afternoon together. It was two hours of flirtatious freestyle, full of jokes, innuendos, and instant familiarity. He could tell he amused Ellen and she wanted to play. He didn't, at least not then. Maybe it was the range of experiences and emotions jammed into such a short time, which had somehow chosen this twilight to descend. Whatever the reason, he felt a kind of gridlock from which response, at least for the moment, was impossible.

Sensing this, Ellen backed off, but not for long.

"I want a priest's opinion," she said with feigned solemnity a few minutes later. "My friends say I have better legs than Kathleen Turner. What do you think?"

"Kathleen who?"

"You know, the American actress in *Body* something— *Meat*, or... "

"*Body Heat*," he corrected her.

"Whatever. What do you think?"

Ellen leaned against the door, stretching her legs, to better define her calves, and pointing her toes. Ben could feel her shoe lightly touch his ankle.

"Well?"

"No," Ben said, in a disinterested monotone David Brinkley would have admired.

"Kathleen, no," he said firmly. "Stansfield, maybe."

"Is Stansfield an actress?"

"Better," Ben assured her, continuing the charade. He then explained that the latter was an old white male who used to head the CIA.

"Asshole," she said as she slugged him on the shoulder.

"You asked," he said, grinning.

Ellen's pique, upon seeing a reaction, proved temporary. She was thinking of a smart reply when the car slowed to a crawl in front of a station manned by armed security guards. Through the dim guardhouse light, Ben could see they were entering a thickly walled compound, more secure than a fort. The tops of the walls were embedded with gleaming, jagged shards of glass.

More so than the guards, who were poor and dark but human, the glass shards offended him. They stood like sentinels, guardians of privilege and separation, deadly as unsheathed knives, but without the mess of human action or emotion.

Ben sat back troubled, wondering about the nature of those who lived within.

"Are there dogs here?"

"Pardon?" The question surprised and disappointed Ellen.

"You know, like German Shepherds and Dobermans."

"No. Tia tried it once, a mixed breed, but it disappeared—probably into somebody's pot."

"What?"

"You know, outside these walls, people eat what they can..."

"Never mind," Ben said. The thought of eating a dog made him uneasy.

He had wondered about that and now he knew. He noticed there were few dogs in the Philippines, and the ones he saw were skinny, pathetic things. They walked tentatively, heads forever peering over shoulders, as if they knew their next step might be their last.

It was part of the legend brought back by American troops after they conquered the Philippines in 1902—Filipinos and dogs, dogs and Filipinos. The relationship shocked the soldiers who, in the defense of canines, slaughtered Filipinos like the dogs the natives ate.

Growing up in the States, Ben had heard the story often enough in different schools in different army towns. For a while, he tried to ignore it. Their family, he always explained, had a dog. Eating her was the last thing on their minds. He felt that his explanation should have settled the matter, burying forever, in the mind of the listener, the evil rumor that Filipinos ate their pets.

It was seldom enough, and Ben, when faced with the invincible ignorance of a classmate, just turned and walked away. He heeded the counsel of Remedios, who abhorred fighting.

In the fifth grade, Ben finally changed his approach.

"Hey, Benny," a tall redheaded boy taunted. "I hear Filipinos eat dogs."

"Look," young Ben explained calmly. "We got a pet dog and we ain't never gonna eat her."

"Just a matter of time, dog eater," the tall redhead said, his smirk saying more than his words.

Ben glanced at his tormentor once, then turned away before reversing direction and pivoting back hard. His clenched backhand—the left, his strongest—was aimed straight at the redhead's smile, which didn't even have time to disappear.

Two seconds later, Ben's target was out cold—two teeth to the minus—and Ben was out of school, suspended for fighting.

At home that evening, Remedios both scolded and soothed

her son by saying that he shouldn't fight and that their pet wouldn't be eaten. At the house that night was Uncle Chris, who tried hard not to laugh.

Chris was a character, one of his parents' lifer soldier friends. As Remedios talked, he grinned evilly, eyeing Harriet, the family mutt named after Ozzie's prim woman. Chris and Remedios went back a long time, to childhood in Cebu and war in the hills.

After an hour or so, Remedios was through with her lecture, and Chris politely waited until she had finished.

"Good with beer," he said gruffly, pointing to the innocent animal. Harriet, otherwise the most courageous of canines, immediately left the room.

Basically, Chris was a good guy, as kind and gentle as any Filipino uncle, except when he drank. And that night, he had drunk too much. Ben's mother and father were seated with him around the kitchen table; his father was imbibing while his mother, as usual, was not.

"Psst," Remedios hissed loudly.

That sound, which young Ben's American ears once heard as some sort of imperfect whistle, was really quite perfect and versatile. Ben eventually came to learn Filipinos used it in a variety of ways—to summon, warn, or, in this case, scold—accompanied by an array of eye, eyebrow, mouth, and head movements. That evening, however, old drunk Chris was beyond warning and even reprobation.

"Oh, come on, Reming," Chris said. "The boy's eleven. It's OK. He should know how Filipinos really are. We survive, Benny, here or there, it don' much matter. The kids got it good here in the States—we all do—but back home, you know, it's hard."

Remedios, struck by the simple truth of Chris's statement, was silent for a moment, allowing him to continue.

"There are times," Chris paused, red-eyed, and turned toward Ben who stood behind his mother, "when if it walks it's cooked. Even Harriet."

"Psst," Remedios hissed again, while furiously raising and lowering her eyebrows. Ben knew it meant he should leave the room, but he ignored the signs, wanting to hear the end of this gruesome tale. Among family, Remedios would simply have told Ben to leave, but Chris's presence changed the equation, by bringing into play her profound sense of *delicadeza*, a trait that seeks avenues of grace, however narrow, in ungraceful situations.

Remedios was reduced to a mad, futile fit of pssting and twitching, and Ben ignored her. He knew that later there'd be the devil to pay—usually in the form of a strap across the back of his legs—but that was later.

Uncle Chris, when drunk, was entertaining and, since his mother's order was implied rather than explicit, Ben could plead cultural ignorance, which Remedios would accept because she didn't want to beat him anyway.

"But Mom," he had said in an earlier successful defense, "I'm American."

So he was, and so he stayed at the table, his mother pssting and twitching like a snake in a frying pan as Uncle Chris continued his morbid Philippine tale.

It began with a question. "Remedios, do you remember the time when Clara's patrol brought back two freshly dead Japs and . . . "

Remedios, knowing the end of the story, was horrified. Chris was on the verge of going much too far. She looked desperately around for help but found none; Albert had passed out, his head slumped on the table.

"Go to your room, Ben!" Remedios said in loud and precise English, her sense of *delicadeza* gone.

Slowly, Ben turned toward his room. A direct order in English—no pleading ignorance on this one.

Chris was so full of booze, he didn't even notice him leave.

"Benny," he heard Chris bellow." You pound the meat long enough, use enough vinegar, it's good as dog. No, better."

In those days, Ben was a quiet kid and a bit small, until he caught his growth at fourteen. Worse, he was unusually shy. His father knew he had little chance of surviving life in army towns unless something was done.

One Friday evening, as Albert was sitting in his usual place—two feet in front of the small black-and-white television in the living room—he turned to Ben.

"Benny," he announced, "you gonna be like Sugar Ray." The weekly fights were on and Sugar Ray was, of course, the great Ray Robinson. Even when pressed, Sugar Ray never seemed to panic, never even sweat, for that matter.

Opposites attract. The principle was never truer than in Albert Lucero's adulation for Ray Robinson, the epitome of style, boxing and otherwise. Whenever he fought and the bout was televised, Albert was there, staring hard at the tiny black vision before him.

On that evening, Sugar Ray was pumping straight and hard left jabs into the face of some artless bruiser. He would then dance lightly around the ring, avoiding his foe's enraged rushes, suffering only the gusts of air as punches sailed harmlessly past their target. What was amazing on this and other Friday evenings was that Sugar's hair never seemed to get mussed. Pompadoured, processed, and slick, there was never a wayward strand. It was always like Sugar Ray, after disposing of his faceless opponents, had more important things to do, like maybe postfight cocktails with Lena Horne.

"Look at that," Albert cackled to Ben, who, despite his exposure to scores of matches, was still unaware of the nuances. "Sugar don' never get his hair mussed."

"Me neither," Ben said solemnly. He was eight years old and wore a crewcut.

"Ah, Benny," Albert said patiently, "it's different. You don' understand.

"You can be like that," Albert added quickly. He was leading up to something and Ben was puzzled.

He looked at his father. "You mean, not get my hair mussed?"

"That," he said, "and more." Albert paused then added quickly, "You know Uncle Sergio?" Sergio Arena was another of Albert's lifer pals. In the Philippines, he had been an amateur boxing champ.

Ben nodded.

"He's gonna teach you, Benny," Albert declared. "And you gonna need it, believe me, skinny and soft as you are. Maybe you be like Sugar Ray?"

"You mean like wearing my hair that way?" Ben asked. He didn't like his crewcut, and the thought of a change in style, even to artificially processed, colored hair, appealed to him.

"No," Albert said, "something better."

Ben's boxing career started shortly thereafter, and it carried through to just before he left for the seminary. In every army town, or wherever the family moved, Albert made sure his son had a good boxing coach, first Sergio, then a host of others.

Ben didn't like it much, particularly at first, but like anything else, he adapted. He was a thin, almost frail boy, and his features dictated his style. Sergio turned him around, fighting him left-handed, teaching him to lead with his right and move continuously away from orthodox, or right-handed, left-leading fighters.

It's a boxing axiom: against orthodox boxers, who are the majority, southpaws are poison. They're awkward, hard to hit, cowardly things, moving constantly away from orthodoxy's thunder—a dangerous and cocked right hand held in close.

In all of his years, Ben was rarely struck with a solid right, and that was fine with him. Fighting became, above all else, a game, and his greatest pleasure came not from belting a foe— he wasn't very mean and didn't have much power anyway— but from making him miss, miss, and miss again.

Away from the gym, his skill as a boxer paid dividends. The black and Mexican kids, despite Ben's inoffensive mien, usually left him alone, allowing him the rare teenage freedom to pick friends and activities. He would spend hours in the library—Remedios insisted—and hang with the boys, even the very bad colored ones. But because he was a boxer and, more important, his mother's son, he would step away before the action got hot or the cops came. Not a word would be said by his friends in protest.

S itting in the car, Ben recalled that he absorbed Chris's story but kept it secret. As a kid, he had known some Japanese Americans in the various army towns. He also had known other Filipinos. He couldn't help but notice a difference between the two. As a whole, the Filipinos were rowdy and, depending on the city and its demography, usually consorted with blacks or Mexicans to wreak different types and degrees of juvenile havoc.

The Japanese, however, were different. They gave no one any trouble. They couldn't, laden as they were with books, rulers, and, Ben assumed, a full list of parental do's and don'ts.

The young Japanese tended to avoid Filipinos. Ben wondered if it was because they knew, or their parents knew, that Filipinos ate them. He couldn't tell, and, as he grew older, its importance disappeared.

D inner with Auntie was a ritual performed hundreds of times before. So why was Ben uneasy?

Back home with his family, and even in Cebu, it meant meals at the fanciest Chinese restaurants. She'd order from the menu in flawless Cantonese, or sometimes even Mandarin. That would impress the waiters, who'd tell the cook.

The cook, who tailored his cuisine to local tastes—in the Midwest it was the Oriental equivalent of hash and eggs— would then produce a splendid feast, often in the middle of some place God farted on and forgot.

Like camels through a needle's eye, a proffering of glazed ducks and steamed fish paraded through doors rarely passed by their kind. Making its way to Clara's table past booths of locals and servicemen, the caravan would elicit quizzical glances and occasional comments from local gourmands.

"Damn," Ben once heard some cowboy drawl, "what's that shit?" The reference was to a steamed bass, cooked whole, eyes dead and bulging.

"Some weird Chinese stuff," came the answer.

"Can't beat this here dish," said the other. "Old Wong fixes it special. Tastes better than Spam and eggs."

Which is what it was, with soy sauce, vinegar, assorted spices, and rice noodles giving it a Chinese flair—so little did the cook, "old Wong," regard his audience.

But with Clara, it was different. Even then, in a foreign land, she was imperious. Clara knew and demanded the best, taking time on more than one occasion to upbraid waiters for sloppy appearance or slow service.

"I don't like Chinamen," Ben once heard her say to his mother, "just their food."

Ben thought the comment was funny, coming as it did from his aunt, whose blood lines, like many from Cebu, were mixed. Her eyes betrayed her, though, disappearing when she laughed.

He had let it pass then, figuring it was just Aunt Clara. But now, as he and Ellen approached the massive oak door of his aunt's mansion, he felt apprehensive. He realized that Clara's contradictions, which he had accepted as a child, were hard to figure. He wondered if he knew his aunt at all.

Ellen led Ben through a long hallway, past expensively furnished rooms, to a brightly lit patio, a stark contrast to the background of black. Overhead, Ben could hear unfamiliar fluttering sounds, close and quickly distant, then silent.

"What's that?" he asked Ellen nervously.

"Bats," she whispered.

"Oh."

Clara was already seated at a finely set table, cigarette in one hand, a glass of wine in the other. She extended her right hand toward him, which he took and pressed to his forehead.

"You're a lucky boy, Nephew, to have the attention of two lovely women."

Ben smiled and slid easily into his chair.

"Maria," Clara called toward the kitchen, "more wine."

Clara was dressed simply, a white open-necked blouse with a tan skirt. Her hair, unfettered, hung down to her shoulders, and Ben, who was used to seeing it in a bun, thought it prettier, more elegant.

To Ben, she cut a striking figure, an aging but still beautiful lioness in her lair. Within these walls, she seemed relaxed and supremely confident, far less acerbic and demanding.

Clara began by regaling Ellen with stories of Ben's youth—
her favorite being how he had once chased Harriet into the
street with her in hot pursuit. Clara fell in front of an approaching car, which screeched to a halt barely in time.

"Even with war," Clara said, "it was the closest I've come
to death. And you know what he did? He walked up to me, that
dumb dog in his arms, and he asks, 'What are you doing on the
ground, Auntie?'"

Clara laughed gently at the memory. She was joined by Ellen, but not by the tale's principal, who blushed.

"But he was such a good boy," Clara added, "very consid-
erate like his mom, even then. I tried to talk Reming into letting him visit me, but she never agreed. I think she was scared
I wouldn't return him."

Clara paused. "Maybe there's still time," she said, winking
at Ben.

Ben shook his head.

"Ah, never mind. The important thing is you're here," Clara
said softly. She looked at Ben and touched his hand. *"Sayang,"*
she sighed, "the circumstances are so sad."

Ben was touched. It was like that all evening, and not as he
had feared. Clara was warm and reminiscent, allowing him a
needed retreat into time—toward something he could always
count on: Aunt Clara, mysterious and constant, showing up
every year, never missing Christmas, never forgetting birth-
days.

At the end of the evening, he bid his aunt goodbye and felt
like a young boy again, which was good enough for him.

The Mercedes was waiting, Junior at the wheel, but before
Ben entered, Clara drew him aside. She said she would be
gone a few days—"to Mindanao"—she added without explanation.

"It's OK, Auntie," he said, "I can. . . "

"Ellen," she interrupted, "will handle my affairs, including your schedule. She'll be over in the morning."

Inside the car, he settled into the comfortable front seat. Ellen, he thought, was a "nice" woman, and he realized then that he was tired, a bit drunk, and had run out of more descriptive adjectives. "Nice" was nice for now.

Earlier, he had wondered whether Ellen would return to the hotel—dangerous speculation for a priest—and what they would do when they got there. In a sense, he was relieved; Clara had detained her. Decisions about adjectives and other matters could wait until tomorrow.

Two rings that morning, the third one was answered.

"Good morning, sir," said the voice on the other end. "A Miss Stansfield Turner expects you in the coffee shop."

Ellen sat in the corner, staring at the bay while savoring a cup of coffee. She wore a pair of white linen shorts and a matching short sleeve shirt. Across her left shoulder was a long strap fastened to an oversized straw handbag. Pretty and perfect, Ellen looked like one of those bored, unearthly models found in *Vogue*.

Ben was nursing a hangover. He was as pleasant as a bear with his foot in a trap. "I don't play tennis," he remarked as he approached.

You should," she said casually without looking up. "Why not?"

"Only white guys play tennis, at least back home when I was a kid. Filipinos throw rocks at each other; you know, real minority sports."

"Oh," she said flatly. "My, you are pleasant. Coffee, Mr. Happy?"

"Sure," he said as he sat down heavily. "What time is it."

"Almost nine, and you're a bad drunk."

There was a tone of admonition in Ellen's voice, and a fear in Ben, however fleeting, that she might leave in a huff.

"Tell me," he nodded, agreeing with her assessment and smiling for the first time, "what's on the agenda?"

"Manila," she said, the cheer in her voice returning. "The entire town. Come on, get ready and I'll show you this place."

By the time Ellen and Ben walked toward the waiting car, a thick, hot, brown-and-black smog had descended, clouding Roxas Boulevard and everything beyond. Ben had seen smog in the States, but this one was worse. It wouldn't disperse, and it seemed impervious to the breeze off the bay that ruffled the back of his blue cotton shirt.

"Great day for tourism," he said sarcastically. "Probably the only place where asthma's fatal."

"You get used to it, Americano," she said, returning the sarcasm. "Now, get in."

With the windows up and the air-con on, Ben stretched and relaxed. As the car crossed Roxas, Ellen put aside her pique and became a tour guide, pointing out sites of potential interest.

"There's Intramuros," she said, directing his attention due east of the hotel.

"It's the old walled Spanish city. Or rather, what's left. The Americans bombed it when they returned, and reduced it to rubble. Some of it's been rebuilt and preserved, but it's not the same.

"And over here's the..."

"Just like this city?" Ben asked, interrupting her.

"Luneta," Ellen said, finishing the sentence. "What did you say?"

"Oh, Mom and Auntie used to say how beautiful all of this once was. No more."

Ellen sighed. "Maybe you're right," she said quietly. *"Sayang.*

"Sayang." she said again.

As Ellen spoke, Junior continued to pick his way gingerly through heavy traffic, past impressive stucco buildings—Ben rightly guessed from their colonial facades they were government offices—next to run-down, dirty storefronts. At each interminable stop, scores of ragged street vendors emerged from the blanket of dust and smoke, invisible until they were upon their targets—occupants of the stalled and waiting automobiles.

"Cigarettes!" cried one who approached the car. He was a slender boy with straw-thin arms. His brown hair had an odd, reddish hue. Ben knew immediately that malnutrition produced that tint; he'd seen it in the texts back home. But now the face of poverty had followed him several thousand miles and was peering into his car window, inches from his own face.

It frightened him.

"No," Ben said to the face, shaking his head, "I don't. . .

"Smoke" was to have been the last word, but he never finished, as the vendor moved quickly to the next car. Ben watched as he worked the line—a market, once moving, created by a stop sign. The delay was compounded by a dead car one block ahead.

Ben noticed the young vendor had in tow a little girl, maybe his sister, tattered as he and brown as a coconut. She was maybe half his size, fragile and small. Like a shipwreck survivor, she clung, in the dusty swirl, to the boy's torn rear pocket. As Ben looked, he noticed her hair also had a faint touch of red. He reached for the lock on the door. It was pushed down, secure, and he made no move to change its position.

Junior saw his chance as a policeman took charge, creating a lane of traffic and waving to him to proceed. He gunned the accelerator, swerving to avoid a driver who had similar intent but slower reactions. The powerful lurch, actually several of them, slammed Ben and Ellen hard against the seat, forward and back again.

"Shit, Junior!" Ellen screamed. That was just the whistle. There followed a long blue train of obscenities and invectives, complete with engine, caboose, and a string of loaded cars.

Poor man, Ben thought, if words could cut, Junior would be dismembered. The "boy" bore it in silence, although Ben could see his knuckles, clenched on the steering wheel, turn from brown to white.

Junior bowed his head as Ellen finally paused to catch her breath. Her outburst had calmed her somewhat, and she sat back red-faced, her right eye twitching from the strain. Fortunately for Junior, the train had stopped in Atchison, not Topeka or Santa Fe.

"Where are we going now?" Ben asked, hoping to switch Ellen's focus.

"Huh?"

"I want to walk," he said as Junior crossed a bridge over a river, broad, brown, and ugly.

"The Pasig," Ellen informed him.

On the other side, the Mercedes slowed then stopped, as traffic, both motorized and pedestrian, converged.

"Here's fine," Ben said, as he reached for the doorhandle.

"Wait," Ellen said, frantically pressing the lock to bar the door.

"You don't understand," she warned. "It can be rough here. Pickpockets, muggers . . . "

"And Tagalog movies," he added cheerfully, pointing to a garish, multicolored display of Manila's latest cinematic effort, *Kapitana Kalibre .45*. It featured three pretty women armed with pistols and automatic weapons. They wore little more than scowls and looked as menacing as the Lennon Sisters.

"Ex-nuns?"

"Look," Ellen said, ignoring the inquiry, "I know this place... "

"Beautiful, semi-naked former nuns," he said in mock rhapsody, "locked in mortal, high-heeled combat. Great. I wish my bishop were here. By the way, what's the name of this wonderful place?"

"Quiapo," Ellen almost shouted. "I used to live here."

"Good," Ben said, smiling. "You can guide me if you like."

With that he was out of the car, making his way to the sidewalk, to the heart of Quiapo. It took Ellen a few seconds to recover. Ben could hear her approaching, breathing hard and muttering curses. He turned to face her, then quickly turned away, hoping to hide his smile.

Junior watched it all; he had no choice. The Mercedes was stuck in traffic. Ellen Labrado was hesitant and stood back, a bit like a child testing the ocean on summer's first day. But Ben Lucero had no such reservations, plunging like a tank into a field of sugar cane. For a second, he disappeared into a multicolored, moving human maze, but he reemerged quickly and extended his hand, which she then took. A moment later, both were gone.

Funny, thought Junior, they look like lovers, a bit like Vic Vargas and Gloria Diaz, his favorite movie stars. He shook his head hard, trying to banish the thought. They were Catholics and, more important, Ben Lucero was a priest. Still, it was hard to tell, particularly the priest. Where's the collar?

No matter, Junior shrugged, none of my business. Not my job. I just drive.

They were in Quiapo for what must have been hours, merging with the crowd when convenient, walking against prevailing currents when necessary. They stopped often, looking at shops and small Chinese restaurants where meats of suspicious origin hung in the display window.

As they strolled, Ben thought he heard Ellen say something. He stopped.

"Pardon?"

"Put your wallet in your front pocket," she whispered. As she spoke, she clung to his upper arm, pulling him toward her with her free hand. Ben bent easily to the side and felt her breasts and belly against his shoulder and arm. Her message complete, she released her grip, but Ben stayed bent too long to go unnoticed.

"Father Ben, I am surprised," she said in mock indignation.

Ben's blush was redder than Rudolph's nose.

"Come on," she said, changing the topic and sparing him further embarrassment. "We'll go in here. They've got air-con and we can get something to drink."

"Here" was a small Chinese café, two doors down from where they stood. Ellen grabbed Ben's hand and moved quickly through the crowd to her destination. She led him to a small booth in the corner.

"I used to come here often," she said, after ordering a beer for Ben and a Coke for herself.

"When was that?"

"Oh, five or six years ago."

Ben was curious about the history of his guide. "What did you do?"

"Studied and worked," she said vaguely. "I'm not from Manila, just like most of the others, I guess. My mom had a bunch of kids, and I was the oldest. So I left and came here."

"That's it?"

"For now," she said coyly, sipping her Coke.

As Ben pondered his next question, he noticed a pretty woman, smartly dressed and about Ellen's age. She was sitting at a table across the room, slightly behind theirs, and was looking toward them. He thought little of it as he shifted his eyes to his companion, who sat next to him on the outside of the booth's bench.

Ben felt relaxed and happy, maybe for the first time since coming to the Philippines. Ellen was smiling, a lovely picture in Ben's mind—even as he watched it flash from peace to pain, then fear and fury.

Ellen was being dragged from the booth by a pair of strong brown hands sunk deep into her hair and she was flung in an instant to the floor. Her attacker—the woman Ben had noticed at the table—then jumped on Ellen, straddling her. The violence was so sudden that Ben froze, watching them grapple for advantage.

A crowd of patrons quickly formed around the two, buzzing excitedly in English and a mix of other dialects and languages. One fellow gestured rapidly with his hand to his companion, signaling a bet on the outcome.

"Better than television!" his friend said in English.

Ben climbed atop the table to peer over the crowd, which by then had blocked his view. His initial reaction, proper for a priest, was to stop the fight. But he didn't. The violence was exciting—dinner theater of a sort, but full of real-life drama—and he was loathe to see it end prematurely.

The women were standing by then, warily circling each other expertly feinting and parrying blows. They exchanged quick jabs and quicker insults. Ben could see they knew how to handle themselves, and this alone spoke volumes about his friend's mysterious background. They seemed equal in size and strength, although Ellen was a bit quicker. Her other advantage was footwear; she wore tennis shoes, while her opponent—"Anita!" he heard Ellen scream on one occasion, "Bitch!" on another—wore medium heels, still not discarded.

"Charge her!" he heard himself advise in a loud voice which, in quick retrospect, embarrassed him. And charge her she did, slipping the next jab off the side of her head as she moved in. Ellen's momentum carried her low into Anita, toppling both to the ground. Ellen was on top, but the other woman had managed to grab her hair and pull her forward, smothering the effect of her punches. Ellen freed herself by raking her enemy's eyes. Finally free, she drew her right hand back and measured Anita with her left. She paused before releasing, as if to savor the impact of a punch that never came.

Ben had jumped off the table and pulled Ellen off. Before anyone could react, they were both out the door running down the street, stopping only from exhaustion, which hit quickly in Manila.

Ellen was near tears. "Goddamit," she spat. "I was really gonna nail that bitch."

"Look," he said in exasperation, "do you want to be arrested? The cops were maybe two seconds away."

"This is yours," he said, handing Ellen her bag. "I grabbed it on the way out."

"Thanks," she said, her left eye starting to swell.

Ben paused. "Who was she anyway?"

"Nobody," she answered sullenly.

"Fine," Ben said. He looked at Ellen, assessing her condition. Aside from her eye, now swollen shut, her nose was bleeding and her lip was badly split.

"You're a mess," he said finally. "We need a place to get off the street and get cleaned up." Junior was long gone, and no taxi was in sight.

"There," he said, pointing to a large, old Catholic Church. "We'll go in there."

Inside the cavernous, dimly lit church, Ben chose a pew near the rear doorway. As Ellen dabbed at her wounds with a handkerchief, Ben scanned the building's interior. He was impressed.

The Spaniards, he thought, were masters of the art of God, a good skill for conquerors. Everything about this church—its size, its dim lighting, everything—stressed God's unlimited power and its corollary, His ability to terrorize. No guitar-strumming Jesus here. Spain's holy friars were agents of a most frightening Lord.

Deep in cynical thought, Ben almost failed to notice they were not alone. Scores of people were spread throughout, hidden in pockets of darkness and buried in prayer, fear, and reflection. Ben knelt, attempting to form an original prayer appropriate for his confusion of recent days. He failed, shook his head in acknowledgment, and resorted to an old formula.

"Hail Mary," he began but didn't finish. He was distracted by a rustling sound behind him, coming down the aisle. Ben turned and saw a toothless old woman, dressed in rags. Her long black veil, longer than herself, dragged after her on the floor. The old woman moved slowly forward on her knees. He looked again; others were moving in similar fashion toward a long box, resembling a casket, set before the distant main altar.

Curious, apprehensive, with growing suspicion, Ben slowly approached the box. Worshippers had already gathered, and those who stood had first genuflected, their hands clasped to their breasts. Others simply knelt, their eyes closed in prayer. The object of their intense veneration was a black, life-size figure of Christ in repose—Mahogany Jesus. To Ben, it carried less spiritual value than the headboard in his hotel room.

"Shit," he whispered as he turned quickly away. Wordlessly, he grabbed Ellen by the arm, almost pulling her out the door.

Ellen was startled. "Where are we going?"

"Anywhere but here," was the angry reply.

As the little red taxi stopped in front of the Manila Hotel, Ben threw a wad of bills at Alex, the driver, and, along with Ellen, jumped out and rushed toward the hotel. In his haste, he didn't bother to count the money, but Alex certainly did. It was four times the regular fare.

Alex smiled and half-wondered if he would advise this American, who looked Filipino, of his error. As he always did at such moments, he polled the small figurines on his dashboard. Mary said yes, Jesus said no, and Joseph, as usual, had no opinion. With no clear majority and, in case of doubt, well... He stuffed the bills into his shirt pocket and drove quickly away, lest the American return and demand a recount.

Money was the last thing on Ben's mind as he and Ellen strode across the hotel lobby and toward the elevators. He just wanted to escape, and his room was his refuge.

Fortunately, the elevator was empty when they entered. Ben noticed that Ellen had donned a floppy white cotton hat and a pair of sunglasses, pulled, he thought, from her bag. The marks of battle were less evident now, although her nose was swollen and her left cheek had darkened noticeably. She was silent and looked straight ahead, although he knew she could hear the thoughts whirring inside his head, questions forming that had not yet been asked. She wouldn't have to answer, but he believed she might. Ellen seemed much like his aunt—blunt, tough, and honest. If Clara was taken with her, he could see why. Maybe he was, too.

"You know," Ben said, breaking the silence, "you can shower in my room, and I'll have dinner brought up. It's been a rough day, and I'd like to get it behind me."

"You've probably got it put together," Ellen said quietly as they walked out of the elevator into the empty lobby. "But you have no right to judge. It takes courage to live here, Americano."

Ben was quiet as he turned the key. He opened the door to his room. "No," he said, shaking his head. "You've got it wrong. I wasn't going to judge—not you or me or anyone else.

Through a window, almost black, the glimmer of ship lights merges with the candlelit reflection of a woman and a man who sit facing each other across a low table. Between them stands a solitary bottle of wine and two half-filled glasses.

The woman is speaking. "Your aunt is very powerful and rich, though I guess you already know that. She owns or controls most of what you see here. I started in one of her places— a massage parlor in Quiapo. I was eighteen then, and for some reason she liked me and brought me to her house about ten years ago. Last year she set me up in another house, one she owns—Banyan Corner Jacaranda, Forbes. It's just down the street from hers." She pauses and smiles before continuing, "For a poor girl, I guess I've done pretty well."

"And your opponent?" he asks.

She laughs. "My rival. She thought the job should've been hers. But she was wrong, though—good body, no brains."

He sits back for a moment, silent.

"And what about you?" she asks.

"It's late," he says evasively, "and there's so much. But there's time, so maybe I'll tell you tomorrow."

He reaches for a nearby light switch. "I'll call Junior," he says in a near whisper.

"Don't," she says evenly, her command keeping the room dark. "Please, I'd like to stay here."

He opens the bathroom door slowly and, from the shaft of light it casts, Ben sees the bed set against the wall. Ellen lies naked on her back, one knee slightly raised. He chooses to keep the dim, narrow light of the doorway, as if its presence postpones the loss of retreat.

There are maybe four steps between where he stands and where she lies. He wonders if the Rubicon was this wide. She is beautiful. About that, and little else, he is sure. Her breasts are full and firm, and her stillness while lying on her back gives her an unusual air of vulnerability. Sea turtles. He is reminded of them, upended on their backs, defenseless against the sun. He knows the thought is ludicrous, but for now an amphibian is his only point of reference. (His mother had made him watch hours of public television and hordes of upended sea turtles.)

He shakes his head, laughing in self-derision.

"Ben," Ellen's voice is quiet, almost timid. He pauses, afraid to answer.

He can see she has turned toward him, her green eyes burning like an iron into his heart. Power once lured Caesar across the river, but tonight the priest is guided by a different muse.

The sounds of passion, of movement and muffled cries, stop suddenly.

"Oh, great," the woman's voice says impatiently.

"What?" Her partner is surprised.

"You missed," she says. "You're on my thigh, on the sheet, and if I turn on the light, you're probably on that too."

"Shit," comes the embarrassed response.

"It's OK," she says, her voice now warm and reassuring. "You're new at this; but the night's long, your cock's nice, and I have time. Call it my part for education.

"Besides," she says, laughing throatily, "after all that abstinence, I'm sure there's a squirt or two left."

If it's his first, a man will awake to study his lover. Early in the morning, but before light, he will wonder if the night lied. Frog or princess? he will ask himself as he slowly traces the lines of her body, unable to sleep until the answer is known.

"Princess," he will say softly to the dark, able now to sleep.

Everyone dreams, even priests. Ben is sitting in a dark night club back in the States. There's a band onstage. He's alone at a table in the back, sipping a beer and taking it in. The lead guitar's burning the first riffs of "Born to be Wild," the rock anthem of the sixties. Ben's not paying much attention, but he soon notices something's wrong.

It's the lyrics. "Born to be mild," sings the lead, followed by the others who repeat the refrain. Ben moves closer—there's something funny about the lead singer—down near the front. The singer is a short Oriental male dressed in a herringbone jacket, slacks, shirt, and tie. Ben recognizes him; he's the psychology professor at Seattle University, a Jesuit school where Ben once took classes.

"Born to be mild," he sings again.

The professor then starts a monologue before introducing his guest. "Just remember," he says solemnly, "that the nail that stands up is the one that gets hit."

He pauses and the crowd murmurs approval.

The music stops, except for a drum roll. "And now," says the professor, "without further ado, fresh from disappointment and death, here's Remedios!"

Ben's mother, beautiful in her wedding gown, takes center stage. "I know you're here, Benny," his mother says. "I'm so disappointed."

Ben stands to speak. "Mom," he says sincerely, "I'm sorry."

She's unmoved. "Sorry's not enough, Ben. What you did was wrong, and my dying's no excuse."

"You've got no control," adds the psychologist. "I've done studies. That's the problem with Filipinos—no caution, no control."

Ben ignores him.

"But Mom," he says, "I'm confused. With you dying and Mahogany Jesus—hell, that's not religion. If it is, maybe I'm not... "

"Without control," the psychologist continues, "you can never be an accountant... "

"Why?" Remedios is crying now.

"Or a priest." The psychologist winks at the band and straightens his tie.

Ben pauses, blinking hard. He loves no one more than his mother, but the moment demands honesty, not deference.

"Why?" Remedios asks again.

"Because I liked it," he says finally.

"I was afraid of that!" she cries as she runs off the stage. "I should have had you neutered!"

Until Armageddon, there will always be a morning after. Ben is awakened not just by the dream, but by a deep soreness in his body that creeps slowly into his mind. Instinctively, he reaches for the woman he had clung to and finds her gone. Eyes still closed, he gropes to his right, then left, thrashing like a fish on the bank. His eyes open. The shades are drawn and the room is dark, an even, black mantle pierced only by the light from a small clock. Six-fifteen, it says, morning or evening he can't tell.

He reaches for a small bedside lamp, hindered by a stiffness that discourages even simple movement. Finally he succeeds and the room is lit. With great effort, he manages to sit up. He runs his hands over his entire body, touching its sorest points. Across his chest there are small red welts. His abdomen feels pulled out of place, the same for his inner thighs and lower back.

On the bedstand, he sees an ashtray full of butts smudged in red. By the tray is a silver lighter and half a pack of cigarettes, American brand. Ellen's, he thinks, although he's never seen her smoke. Hope in odd places? The nearby mess comforts him; traces of love and thought. I'm not, he thinks, just a fuck.

Ben reaches again, and again pulls against muscles that contract. Succeeding, he lights a stick, coaxing air into lungs where smoke has never been.

Before tonight, or maybe it's morning, he had wondered what lovemaking was like. Now he knows and isn't sure what it means. He has, it seems, always been a priest; it is what he has wanted. At its best, it has given him a sense of purpose—that of serving God and man—and until Ellen, it was his calling, never questioned. He wonders what his professors and the older priests might say, how they would advise. But he believes he knows the answer.

One or the other, Ben, they'll say. Flesh or spirit. You are chosen, and to be chosen means to make choices.

Choices, a word he now fears. It was once so easy. He thought he had chosen the priesthood, but maybe not. He had felt no pang or remorse in surrendering one life, which he really didn't know, for another, which he did. He loves his vocation, but can't condemn what has happened.

He draws another puff and notices only the filter is left. He stubs it out and flings it across the room in the direction of a wastebasket.

He understands he must choose, but not here in Manila, where the rules of order seem suspended. All he knows is that he's tired, terribly so. Sliding under the covers, his last thoughts are of Ellen—when she'll call and when he'll see her. He hopes it's soon.

Come on, Ben," a voice said softly. A hand on his shoulder rocked him gently, like a child in a cradle. A light pushed against his closed eyelids, and he closed them tighter. Ben felt the covers being quickly withdrawn, and with it their warmth. Instinctively, he reached forward to catch them but failed. He then curled like a fetus, his back to the voice and his hands covering his genitals.

"Modesty becomes you," the voice said with a laugh, which Ben suddenly recognized.

He opened his eyes. "Ellen!" he said, unwinding from his curl. Ben sat up, swung his feet to the floor, and stretched. To his surprise, the stiffness was gone.

"How'd you get in?"

"Erasmo," she explained, referring to the bellman.

"How long have I been sleeping?"

"About a day and a half," she said. "I would have loved to have stayed," she paused and winked, "but some of us must work."

Ben smiled. "I wish you could have."

"Oh, Ben," she said in an admonishing, gently mocking tone, "that's not a proper wish for a priest."

He started to blush.

"Did you," Ben stammered, "I mean, was I . . . "

Ellen sensed an opening—the eternal morning-after question—and moved deftly in. "No," she said evenly. "You were enthusiastic."

It wasn't the answer Ben wanted. He was mortally wounded, cut beyond his psychic quick.

She also sensed her overkill. "Oh, Sweetie," she said contritely, "joke only. You were good and getting better. Talk about missionary position. I'd be sleeping, or trying to, and then wake up with you on me, pumping like a Nissan piston."

"Ellen, I don't remember." Ben continued blushing, this time for a different reason.

She went on, ignoring his disclaimer. "Your dick's under warranty, right? Bionic, battery-operated, Duracell."

Ben was quiet. His normal color was slowly returning.

"Look," he said haltingly. "I don't want to talk about my dick."

"Hah!" she said cynically. "That's a first."

The comment irritated Ben. "Look," he said. "Don't lump me with others. I just don't want to talk about it, at least not this way."

Ellen turned and walked toward the window. Stopping, she gathered her thoughts. "You pleased me, Ben," she said slowly. "Is that important to you?"

He nodded his head. "Yes,"he mumbled.

Ellen turned to face him. "I'm glad," she said.

Ben stared at her and paused. He felt her green cat eyes, dangerously clear in the daylight. A look of uncertainty crossed his face, and in that moment, he broke for safety.

He stood up abruptly, "I need to shower and get out of here."

Ellen wasn't buying. "Do you want company?" she asked,

unfastening her sandals and walking toward him.

Ben was silent and motionless, arms folded protectively across his chest.

"Remember, cleanliness and godliness," she continued brightly, "and fun with soap."

Still silent, Ben continued looking at her. She was barefoot and her light cotton dress clung nicely to her hips and breasts.

"Look," she said with exaggerated impatience. "Do you want me to beg?"

He turned away toward the bathroom door, his hidden smile stating the obvious. Begging wasn't necessary.

Off Manila Bay blew a brisk afternoon breeze, providing relief for those lucky enough to be along the shore. It lifted the smog from Roxas Boulevard, pushing it inland and away from tourists, squatters, and others whose business, serious and not, brought them there. Among the fortunate were Ellen and Ben, walking slowly and together without purpose or direction, as lovers have always done. His long right arm was draped across his companion's shoulders; his hand rested lightly on her collarbone.

"Aesthetics," he said quietly.

"Pardon?"

"Nothing," he said. "Just something Aunt Clara once told me."

As they walked, he let his hand casually slip to Ellen's breast. His fingers strummed her nipple like a guitar. It grew erect and supple like a mushroom stalk. "Nice," he said, admiring the result.

"Stop," she said firmly, squirming like a six-year-old from his grasp. "Not in public," she whispered.

Her protest mildly surprised him, but he ignored her and moved closer, and his hand extended to reclaim his position.

Quickly, Ellen grabbed his thumb, twisting it upward, away from his palm.

"OK! OK!" Ben shouted through clenched teeth, pain racing up his arm.

She released the pressure, placing Ben's arm snugly around her waist, and continued walking. Through the brief commotion, they hadn't broken stride.

More than a thumb was momentarily out of joint. Ben was pouting, although he tried to laugh it off, and she moved quickly to repair the damage.

"It's mostly me," she explained calmly, attempting to soothe him. "When I worked, men always thought they bought me. But they were wrong. My services maybe, but never me. On my back on a bed with the doors closed, OK. But never in public." She nodded at the people on the sidewalk. "Not their business," she said. "Can you understand?

"Can you?" she repeated, and squeezed Ben around his waist.

Ben nodded yes.

"In your world," she continued, "people like you judge people like me. In your eyes, whores have no standards. But I did."

Ben nodded again, somewhat reflexively. He didn't fully understand her pique—couldn't have—but he was trying. Ben felt ashamed. He wasn't like other men; he respected women, or at least that's what he thought and preached and counseled. Remedios had made sure of that. But now his mother was gone and maybe, too, the comfort of self-deception.

Ben stopped walking and stepped away from Ellen. Like Muhammad Ali from Frazier, he needed time and the safety of distance. He fumbled for words, treating English like a foreign tongue. "Ellen," he stammered, then paused, unable to continue. "Ellen," he began again, and again could go no further.

South of where they stood he heard the sharp sound of angry voices and maybe gunfire; he wasn't sure. The distant noise rose above the din of Roxas Boulevard, rolling like a carpet over everything in its way. Along the boulevard, a few of the curious ran forward to inspect. Most, however, walked or ran in the opposite direction, fleeing the sound and the danger it represented.

Ben looked at Ellen, confusion marking his face; then he headed quickly toward the commotion. He was several yards gone, having just started to trot, when a firm hand seized his elbow. It was Ellen.

"Ben," she said, gasping for breath, "stay away. It's not your fight. It's dangerous. You don't understand."

"Let go," he said, shaking free. "I've got to go."

He quickened his pace, briefly reaching a sprint then slowing again to a trot. He looked back. Ellen was still there, and he turned quickly to wave.

"See you at the hotel," he shouted.

The sound of conflict was not much farther ahead, maybe three hundred meters. He could see a large crowd surging forward and being pushed back. Their object was a white stucco building set near the edge of the bay. Surrounding it was a metal fence, ringed on the outside by khaki-clad Metro-Manila police. Within the compound was an indelible mark of identification—a long pole atop which flew an American flag. (Another American flag was burning in the street.) Ben immediately knew the besieged building was the U.S. Embassy.

Closer now, he started to walk, and he noticed the largest group of police guarding the embassy gate. Behind them, within the compound area, were scores of American Marines, their weapons drawn. Stationed behind barricades, they were poised and ready to fire.

From Ben's vantage, now closer then caution would dictate,

he could see that some of the defenders had already moved forward, their long riot sticks swinging in all directions. He moved even closer and could hear the thud of truncheons finding their marks, followed by the screams of the injured. The protestors—Ben thought there were a thousand, maybe more—greatly outnumbered the police.

A trace of tear gas, weak where Ben stood, burned his eyes. Still, the crowd pressed on, many now covering their faces with bandanas and shirts. The police were losing ground, their foes forcing them against the embassy gate, which shook and bent as bodies were thrown and pinned against it.

Suddenly, above the din, Ben heard a single sharp retort, followed by a long burst. He dove to the sidewalk, face to the side, then looked up to determine the direction of the shots. It wasn't the Marines; they had held their fire, their fear and surprise equal to his.

One fell, then another, and what had once been a continuum of movement and direction suddenly became something else as people fled in panic. Roxas was soon clear and, from the distance, Ben could see soldiers advancing, their bayonets fixed, toward what was once the scene of battle. Those left behind were the dead and wounded.

Ben's legs shook as he forced himself to stand, and he felt a warm dampness in his pants. He closed his eyes, trying hard to control the fear that now consumed him.

"Strength, Jesus!" he screamed to a God he had all but forgotten as he ran ten meters to the nearest body. Quickly, he turned it over—a young boy, dead. Nearby was someone else—a young man, badly wounded but showing signs of life. Ben ran to his side.

"I'm a priest," Ben shouted, waving off a pair of approaching soldiers. The older one, a sergeant, nodded to his companion; they passed without comment.

Ben turned his attention to the man on the ground. His face was bloody, as was his shirt, a bullet having entered below the rib cage. Ben stripped quickly, using his own shirt to compress the open wound. Although Ben was no doctor, he could tell the man was dying. Not long for this world, he thought. Blood covered the man's forehead and eyes, and pain twisted his features. He was breathing in gasps, exhaling, on each labored occasion, a thin, bloody spray.

"I'm a priest, son," Ben said softly, as he used his fingers to wipe some of the blood from the man's face. The wounded man opened his eyes and, as he did, Ben recognized him.

"I know you," the man said weakly. "I work with Erasmo at the hotel. You're Ben."

Ben blushed. For a guilty moment he thought of asking the dying man what he knew about him, about him and Ellen.

"Hell!" Ben mumbled, bending again over the man.

"I'm not good, eh Ben?"

"Are you a Catholic?" Ben asked.

The man nodded affirmatively.

Ben said, "I'll administer the last rites."

The dying man laughed, his effort causing him to wheeze and spit up blood. He shook his head no, then motioned Ben closer.

"A real priest, Benny," he said. *"Get me a real priest."*

B en slumped in his chair, unable to move. Hand over his eyes, he faced the bayside window, now black, and saw nothing.

He expected Ellen to call or visit, but he wasn't sure what to say. His bag was packed, and his ticket and passport lay on the edge of his bed. He was flying standby for the States early tomorrow morning.

Aunt Clara had not returned, and for that he was thankful.

She would insist—"One more day, Ben," she'd say—and he didn't want to argue. The Philippines was too far beyond him, and now his only wish was to leave. For the first time since arriving, he thought of home—a sanctuary much safer than the madhouse he had entered—and how he longed for Seattle's cool air, clean streets, and pronounced sense of order. Dad had mustered out there, and the family stayed.

Ellen? He couldn't face her, either. She had raised questions for him—had made visible an otherwise unseen side—but these would be sorted out away from Manila. He knew he was running, and he was ashamed. Ellen deserved better, but there was so little of him left.

A note, maybe. At least a note. He reached for a pad and pen on a nearby table and started to write. "Dear Ellen" was as far as he got. He would write, he told himself, in the States.

In was 9:00 P.M., dangerously late for an unencumbered, or so he hoped, retreat. He rose from the chair and gathered his few belongings. He then opened the door, scanning the room once more before turning off the light. So much, he thought, had taken place here, and a sense of sadness touched him briefly.

"Please understand and forgive," he whispered, as he reached for the switch.

The door closed, and he stepped into the hall. "Bellman," he said to a young boy standing by a desk. "Call me a cab. I'm checking out tonight."

"Yes, sir."

In the hallway, Ben could hear the muffled ringing of his telephone, then silence. He turned toward the waiting elevator, memories carried into the night.

PART V

— 8 —

Angelo and Muhammad

After clearing customs at Sea-Tac, Ben walked quickly to the passenger pick-up area. Teddy was there, waiting. Ben had cabled him from Manila the morning of his departure. He spotted a cherry-red 1975 Caddy Seville double parked in the airporter loading zone. Typical Teddy. He was hard to miss.

"Hey, Angelo!" Teddy shouted, after spotting Ben in his rear-view mirror. "Welcome back!"

It was Ben's childhood nickname, and he replied in kind. "Muhammad!" The response evoked a broad smile on Teddy's dark Filipino face. They went back many years, their fathers having served in the army together. Both fathers had mustered out at about the same time and had chosen Seattle to raise their families. Ben and Teddy played together and attended—until Ben left for the seminary—the same schools.

Teddy was shorter than Ben, but heavier, packing 175 pounds in a compact, powerful frame. Although Ben had his share of childhood fights, Teddy was more aggressive and far more successful, so much so that even the black kids thought twice about challenging him.

Teddy's build dictated his fighting style, but during one bout with a tall Indian boy, Teddy abandoned his usual bullish tactics to mimic the arrogant grace of Muhammad Ali. To Ben it seemed comical, almost absurd, a bit like Sonny Liston doing Fred Astaire. He worked hard to suppress a giggle. But Teddy, whose instincts were keen, could afford the switch, having earlier sealed the contest's outcome by leading with a rock to his opponent's face. The blood flowed into the Indian's eyes, rendering him helpless before Teddy's stylistic onslaught.

"Ali!" the crowd of eighth-graders shouted as he danced, pumping hard and precise left jabs into his sightless opponent. "Ali!" The nickname stuck.

"I guess I'm Muhammad," Teddy told Ben shortly afterward. "Cool. That's one slick dude.

"I'm Muhammad and you're Angelo," he added, honoring Ben with the name of Ali's famous trainer, Angelo Dundee.

From then on it was Muhammad and Angelo. "Don't mess with Angelo, motherfucker," Teddy warned potential predators on more occasions than Ben could recall. And, for the most part, they didn't.

The boys were inseparable, unlikely a pair as they were, until 1964, when Remedios, over Muhammad's ill-concealed sulk, dispatched Angelo to St. Andrew's, the local seminary.

Teddy was never religious, but his parents were. They adorned their home with a variety of Catholic icons, including a five-foot statue of Jesus—one hand raised in greeting, the other pulling back his robe to reveal a blood red heart crowned with thorns. It stood by the front door, routinely shocking the unwarned and discouraging Girl Scouts, salesmen, and an occasional burglar.

Teddy was immune to his environment. He often wound his

jockstrap around Jesus's upraised fingers, leaving it on just long enough for his mother to notice and scream in protest.

Although Ben would return for summer breaks and seek out his friend, something had changed. Teddy deeply resented Ben's vocation and the breakup of their partnership. He had made this clear Ben's first time back.

"Come on, Ben," Teddy said, using his real name to underscore the conversation's gravity. "You goin' queer or what?"

Wisely, Ben didn't respond. He just walked away. The contacts with Teddy grew fewer, until one day Remedios called and said Teddy had enlisted, U.S. Army, destination Vietnam.

Vietnam. It hit the old neighborhood hard, like a plague that swept a village. But it was specific in its choice of victims: colored males, eighteen and older, poor. The one possible antidote was a magical four-year college deferment, but so few from the neighborhood, graduates and victims of public education, even knew where the colleges were, much less how to apply and be accepted, that the antidote was illusory, never real.

In the late 1960s, as the war heated up and more were summoned to feed the fire, Remedios would call and tell Ben who was drafted, wounded, missing, or dead. For her, it was a roster of sorrow, mournful and profound, cutting deep her mother's heart. Ben listened patiently, but for him, it was something less—a recital of names removed from feeling. Some were familiar, others not.

In those days, moved more by love for her son than concern for his calling, Remedios would end with a warning. "Stay there, Benny," she would say. "Please stay there."

On that point, Remedios need not have worried. Ben liked school, loved it, in fact. Sylvan and serene, St. Andrew's was at the northern edge of Lake Washington, miles from his old neighborhood, worlds removed from his past.

Ironically, Ben's first assignment was to his old parish, St. Mary Immaculate. During his years away, the congregation had changed—fewer blacks and Japanese and more Filipinos, mostly recent immigrants. In the archbishop's mind, assigning Ben there made perfect sense—a Filipino face for a Filipino church.

For Ben, however, the archbishop's logic was less compelling. He had no experience with *recent* immigrants and spoke none of their dialects. He understood just one—Cebuano— badly. Ben didn't think he disliked immigrants; his mother, after all, was an immigrant. He just thought, or so he told himself and others, that the language gap was too wide. Remedios and the parents of his friends, immigrants all, had at least the benefit of decades in the new land, and their English, however poor, was at least understandable. The same couldn't be said of the newcomers.

His dissent sounded so good, so reasonable, that those who heard him would invariably agree. But there was an incident in Ben's past he chose not to relate, or remember.

In the sixth grade, a young Filipino, "fresh off the boat," joined their class. All eyes focused on Celso, his every move and comment. His presence made the other Filipino students nervous, even hostile. During English period, as the class worked on a writing assignment, Celso raised his hand.

"Mu'm," he said meekly to the teacher. "I want to go to the cum-port room."

Everyone listened and watched intently, and one little black girl sitting behind Celso heard every word.

"Cum-port, cum-port," she whispered, wickedly mimicking his accent. "He wants to pee-pee in de cum-port room." Others heard her, including the American-born Filipinos, who were anxious not to be part of an accent and manner of speech so foreign and strange. They soon took the lead in taunting the newcomer.

Poor Celso endured for almost the entire school year, but he was expelled in early May for trying to stab Teddy with a knife brought from home. He failed, but the attempt left upon its intended victim a lasting impression.

"Those FOBs are different," he said to Ben, who nodded in agreement.

Despite his doubts, recognized and hidden, Ben took the job at St. Mary's; new priests have little cachet to do otherwise. Starting as an assistant, he soon succeeded the old pastor, who died upright in the confessional. That was three years ago.

It was three years ago, too, that Teddy reappeared after more than a decade. The last Ben had heard, he had mustered out in California. Teddy's mom had since died, his brothers had moved out of town, and his father had returned to the Philippines. Ben expected to see him at the funeral, but he didn't show, and family members were mum on his whereabouts.

Teddy just appeared unannounced, ragged and thin, one clear, cold morning at the rectory door.

"Angelo," he said simply.

Ben overcame his shock and quickly invited him in. After a cup of coffee and halfway through a Salem, Teddy started to talk. He said that after Vietnam, he just kicked around, unsure of everything. There was crime, some jail time, bad drugs, a failed marriage, and two kids—he thought it was two, but wasn't sure—who hated his sight. It was clear Teddy needed help, which Ben couldn't refuse.

"Stay here," Ben offered. "I need typing, repair, maintenance, and painting. The pay's not much, but there's room-and-board, and you can stay until there's something better."

Teddy smiled, his features untypically hawklike and sharp. "You the boss," he said after a deep drag.

"One thing, though," Ben added solemnly. He stood silent for a moment, his eyebrows arched. "No jocks on statues, OK?"

Something better never came, and Teddy stayed at St. Mary's. A year ago, he bought the Cadillac from Theo, a dark, thin, extremely nervous brother from the neighborhood. Teddy and Theo knew each other from high school. They had run together and had hooked up again when Teddy returned to his old haunts.

Even as a boy, Theo had his own peculiar set of dreams. "Check that dude out," he said to Teddy, pointing out a nicely dressed pimp behind the wheel of a long, sleek, gas-eating American car.

"Brother got it made," he added. "Got ladies with big butts, big legs, and fake hair workin' for him. He don't do shit but kick back and collect."

Teddy knew the man Theo had pointed to. His name was Willy—a hard case, stone killer, ex-con, whose hair had been artificially straightened.

"Forget it," Teddy tried to argue. "Willy's bad and you ain't, and that's a fact."

Theo paused, offended by his friend's assessment. "You ain't born bad," he finally said. "You learn it. And I can learn it."

"Yeah, sure," Teddy said.

"And besides," Theo continued, "I don't aim to be bad as Willy. A moderate level of badness and income's OK. Brother Willy's what you might call upwardly mobile."

Theo waited for his discourse on finance to sink in. "The mobility I seek is lateral."

"Yeah, sure," said Teddy, unconvinced and unimpressed.

But Vietnam had crushed even that modest aspiration. Theo's second day on patrol, he stepped on a mine, losing part of his right kneecap. When he returned to the neighborhood, he tried a series of straight jobs—store clerk, postman, carpenter's apprentice—and found them wanting. His dream still survived, so he took his savings, investing them in a used red Caddy and a closet full of new clothes. Shortly thereafter, he was on the streets, a future prince of capitalism and Seattle's newest black entrepreneur.

Teddy was right. Theo's bluster carried him for a while—he always could talk—but like fossil fuel, it was soon running low. He was just never hard enough, not on his women, or other pimps, or customers. And although he packed a piece—a two-inch, .38-caliber Smith and Wesson—he hated confrontations. He once drew down on another pimp but couldn't squeeze, and the word was soon out. The "pimp with a gimp" was a lion without claws, unable to defend what he claimed to be his.

Only the vice-cops loved Theo, since his mild (by criminal standards) manner meant an easy, nonviolent bust good for statistics. He had it the morning he called Teddy at the rectory. That afternoon, he was to be arraigned on a variety of charges, some relatively serious, that he intended not to hear.

"Say," Theo said over the phone.

"Theo," Teddy replied, recognizing the voice. Teddy's legion of black friends never identified themselves; that job was his.

"Fixin' to split," Theo explained. "The ride's yours for $900."

All I got's seven," Teddy said. "Take a check?" he asked facetiously.

"Get serious," Theo said, irritated. "Do I look like a bank?"

"OK, OK," Teddy said. "Heat?"

"Serious heat," Theo answered.

"Then $600 tops," Teddy said.

How was Manila?" Teddy asked, as Ben slid into the front seat.

"Just like St. Mary's," he said.

"Nuts?"

Ben nodded as Teddy pulled the Cadillac smoothly into traffic.

"Too many Filipinos, huh?"

"Face it, Angelo," Teddy said emphatically. "There's a world of difference between them and us."

Them and us. It was that way with Teddy. Ben expected it and let it pass. "How's the parish?" he asked, hoping to change the topic.

"Not too cool," Teddy solemnly replied. "You know Artie, Mrs. Del Rosario's youngest boy?"

Ben nodded. "Sure," he said.

"Got his head kicked in."

"What!" Ben was shocked. Cora Del Rosario and his mother were old friends—*kumadres*, in fact—and Artie was Remedios's favorite godson. He was several years younger than Ben but, like him, American-born. Although he hadn't seen Artie for a while—he'd enlisted in the army two years ago—the news hit him hard.

Cora and his mother's friendship dated from the Luceros's arrival in Seattle. Cora had heard through the extensive and accurate Filipino grapevine that a new Filipino family was coming to the neighborhood. Shortly after the moving truck pulled into the driveway of the small, three-bedroom frame house, Cora was at their doorway, carrying a large tray laden with *lumpia*, *puto*, and other Filipino treats.

"It's not much," she said then, "but please—we know how it is—please, feel welcome."

Stunned by the news of Artie, Ben remembered that day more than twenty years past. He remembered, too, that Cora was always there for the Luceros, like when his parents died a year apart, first Albert, then Remedios. Each time, it was Cora who brought comfort and wisdom. Brought also was her promise, unstated but real, that such burdens would be shared, as they always are by Filipinos. Ben could still hear Cora's voice, and, with his hand lightly touching his chest, he felt with numbing clarity the pain she now felt in her heart.

He shuddered and shook his head. "Wha. . . ," he stammered, "what happened?"

He came home on leave and was down in Chinatown," Teddy said, "Filipino bar. Three dudes jumped him."

"Well, how's he . . . "

"Not good," Teddy cut in grimly, anticipating the question. "Still alive, at least this morning, but they've pulled the plug."

"Shit," Ben whispered as he slumped in his seat, his face drained of blood. He looked onion-white.

Teddy continued. "No one's talkin', but everyone knows." Teddy paused and looked at his friend.

"FOBs, brother," Teddy said. "FOBs."

That same day, Ben went straight to St. John's—the hospital where Artie lay, not alive but not yet dead. Cora, upon seeing him, hugged him and sobbed uncontrollably while Manong Severo, Cora's husband, sat in a corner staring at a glass of water brought by a nurse. Other family members either sat or stood around, the men with hands in their pockets, the women seeking solace in rosary beads or missals.

Ben looked at Cora and tried to say something soothing, but he couldn't find the words. He would look at her and think of

Remedios, how she might have handled this, had it happened to her. No different, he thought sadly.

Among Filipinos, sorrow, once released, flows like a river without a dam. Artie soon died and was buried. As a priest, Ben had buried many, but this death was different for him, its anguish more deeply felt.

At the funeral, the casket stayed closed. The wounds were too garish for repair and public review. One by one they filed by, family first, until Cora, wearing the black lace of sorrow, arose from prayer and entered the aisle. Her sobs soon filled every crevice in the half-filled church. As she neared her son, her legs shook and she fell on one knee, an involuntary genuflection. Rising, she made it to the communion rail but no farther. She knelt there and cried her sad goodbye.

Along with Cora's sons and daughters, Ben rushed forward to assist. She shooed each of the others away until only the priest was left, dressed in his vestments of mourning. Slowly, Cora composed herself, allowing Ben to help her back to her pew. As they walked slowly, Cora leaned on his arm and pulled him close.

She whispered in Cebuano, "I'm glad it's you, Benny, you burying my boy. You'll take care of him."

Cora's words cut the Gordian knot of doubts hidden in Ben's heart. They summarized in a nutshell what he loved most about his job. In Manila he'd come close to losing it, but back home, the reason he had become a priest was again unmistakably clear. It helped that Ellen was there and not here, clouding the question. Priests were only men, his confessor said; they'd fallen before. He wasn't the first or the last. What was needed now was commitment, in his case, re-commitment to a promise—the choice made years ago—that

God's way, by definition, precluded others. The wonder, Ben thought, was that God still loved him.

He was alone in his study. It was near midnight, and only a small lamp provided light for eyes grown heavy with sorrow and reflection. It was enough for Ben to sit at his desk, pen in hand, to finish a chapter just recently started.

"Dear Ellen, . . . " it began.

After mass the next morning, Ben walked to a mail box a block away from the rectory. Pulling the handle, he placed Ellen's letter inside and paused for a moment as he watched the thin, blue air-mail envelope resist gravity, lingering on the incline before disappearing. He released his grip and turned toward the rectory, ignoring a powerful surge of sadness which, had it happened in Manila, would have kept him there.

For him, the episode was over, and he hoped Ellen would understand. He had made his peace, if not with her, then at least with himself. Life for them both must continue. Ben wanted to reimmerse himself in the routine of parish life—masses, baptisms, and the like—the staples of priesthood. St. Mary's wasn't always this hectic, and death wasn't always so violent or traumatic.

His routine would return, he told himself as he neared the church, and this morning its first sign would be a fresh pot of coffee and the daily paper.

Like a young colt, he quickened his pace, gradually breaking into a near gallop. The rectory's steps loomed ahead and he intended to bound several at a time. Effortlessly, he cleared the first four, but a car pulled up and a shout from behind froze further movement.

"Benny!" it said. "Father Ben!"

Ben recognized the voice and felt panic in his gut. He remained motionless, facing the rectory's front door.

"Godammit, Ben," the voice said impatiently. "Turn around. There's not much time."

Slowly, Ben obeyed. It was Johnny Romero, policeman and St. Mary's messenger of bad news. Johnny was a *mestizo;* his dad was an alcoholic ex-fighter from Ilocos Sur. His mother, whom Ben had never met, was some kind of Indian—it was never clear—maybe Alaska Native or Coastal.

Ben knew Johnny as a kid and, when Johnny wasn't in reform school, he lived with an older half-brother in a small apartment a few blocks down from Ben's parents' house.

In those days, there were a lot of mixed marriages that typically involved young immigrant Filipino males with any available female. Half of Ben's peers were mixes of some kind, despite a variety of legal and social bans on interracial sex. This, according to Teddy during one of his eighth-grade flashes of insight, proved that Filipinos were friendly and would poke anything that moved.

For a lot of mixed bloods, though, there's sometimes a price, and Johnny paid his. As a kid, he ran exclusively with other Filipino Americans who lived around St. Mary's. Come the sixties and the surge of federal education programs, and Johnny discovered the benefits of his other heritage. He was recruited to the University of Washington, sustained on the largesse of the Bureau of Indian Affairs and Lyndon Johnson's Great Society, and turned on to a culture he really didn't know.

One summer back from the seminary, Ben bumped into Johnny in Chinatown. He didn't recognize him. Johnny had grown his hair long and braided it, Indian-style. Later, a mutual friend said Johnny'd gone total Indian. "He's hoppin' around at powwows," marveled Lenny, a Filipino guy Johnny used to run with. "Yells like he's got a stick up his ass. But the sucker wins. He throws in some funky little dance step never seen on the res' and it just blows 'em away. Makes 'em crazy, too."

He added that Johnny knew that real Indians resented him, but he couldn't have cared less. Agency money was good, and besides, the only thing Filipino blood ever got him was warnings from Japanese parents to their pubescent and impressionable daughters: Don't smack those lips for Johnny R.

Johnny loved college. He could dance and screw, courtesy of the BIA, and not have to worry about money. But soon the incompletes caught up, so out he went to a civil service exam and—despite his youthful errors (stricken when he hit eighteen) and, because of the blind application of affirmative action—he landed feet first, hired by the city police. Ironically, part of his beat was his old neighborhood and, back in familiar surroundings, Johnny was Filipino once more.

Ben wasn't surprised by Johnny's choice of profession. It had happened before; a lot of Filipinos became policemen, just like other Asians became accountants. They liked the badge and the blue, somber suit. And they loved the gun. But Ben figured these were just outer trappings. The real reasons lay within.

There was something else, something in their culture, however diluted it was by life in America, that allowed wild swings in cruelty and compassion, that paid tribute to authority—youthful rebellion aside—yet tolerated, even glorified, violence.

For guys like Johnny, this was as good as it got—an adolescent extension, but secure and reasonably well paid, and this time played on the winning side.

C ome on, Ben," Johnny shouted. "This one can't wait."
Jarred by the urgency of the command, Ben quickly entered the car on the passenger side.

"Fasten your seat belt, Padre," he said, as he flipped the switch for the flashing blue lights. "We goin' for a ride."

"What's up?" Ben asked, as he braced his palms against the dash.

"Double murder," Johnny answered, staccato-style. "Heard it on the radio. One survivor, critical.

"Barkada," he added.

Ben sank in his seat. *Barkada.* It was a Filipino word that even Filipino Americans came to know. Loosely translated, it meant a person's peer group, his point of reference that commanded and received loyalty, often blind loyalty.

In the Philippines, geography's curse was a territory split into seven thousand islands, overwhelming its people with isolation and a pervasive sense of vulnerability. There *barkada* made sense. One alone could hardly survive, indeed, wasn't expected to. So Filipinos banded together on the basis of common traits, real and imagined. The resultant outlook was as tribal and fractured as that once held by the Hatfields and Mc-Coys.

Over here, though, it was supposed to be different. But habits don't disappear with a change of residence or nationality; sometimes not even with the passage of time and generations. Even though Ben's friends were all American-born and English-speaking, they could still resemble their immigrant parents.

As the car weaved through the narrow, rutted streets surrounding St. Mary's, Ben thought of Teddy. Despite Teddy's aversion to immigrants, he was the most tribal of all and, in that sense, the most Filipino. Routinely he'd go to the wall for any friend, a practice that found him on the wrong end of sticks, knives, and an occasional gun. To Teddy, though, it didn't matter, and when Ben asked him once to explain, he simply said, "Got to."

"Got to" said it all, Ben thought. No doubt the same dynamics applied here—a cycle of violence triggered by Artie's death. His suspicions were soon confirmed.

"You know that Del Rosario killing?" Johnny asked, without turning to look at Ben. He knew the answer.

"Yeah," Ben said.

"Shit's connected," Johnny said. "We know who jumped Artie, but two are still out. The folks that got it—they live in South Seattle—are one of the suspects and his parents. We haven't caught the others—his older brother and a cousin—but we will."

"The boy's at St. John's, still alive," Johnny added, "but not for long. We need your help, Benny."

Ben was irritated. "Hey," he said. "It's not my job. Anything this kid—what's his name?"

"Arsenio."

"Anything Arsenio tells me in confession, I can't tell you."

"Cool, Benny," Johnny said calmly. "I'm not asking for that. I know the rules. Just get him to cooperate with us. Besides, he's gonna die, and he'll save the State some money. I don't need his confession."

Ben was silent.

Johnny continued, encouraged by Ben's lack of objection. "You know how Filipinos are. Just tell him the cops will do his payback. You know, vengeance. He'll like that."

"Johnny," Ben said quietly, breaking his silence. "How do you know Arsenio's Catholic?"

To Johnny, the question was absurd, its answer self-evident.

But it surprised him. For a moment, he looked confused. "Get serious," he said finally, after clearing his throat. "All Filipinos are Catholic."

Johnny was right. Arsenio was Catholic and anxious to confess. He was even more anxious to punish his assailants. One of the .45-caliber slugs lodged near his heart, making the wound inoperable. It was just a matter of time, or so the doctor said.

As Ben sat at Arsenio's bedside, hearing his confession, he looked down at the bandaged form, slender and vulnerable. Suddenly, Ben was seized by a powerful, black revulsion. Arsenio's salvation lay in a timely apology—"Sorry. Sorry. Goodbye."—that Ben was part of. Arsenio had killed the son of Ben's mother's friend. The thought of Arsenio entering heaven sickened him.

Murderer, Ben thought. Immigrant greaseball. Find your own way through the needle's eye. Teddy was right. Two tribes, them and us; the twain never meant to meet. Sucker, you deserved it.

Overcome, Ben looked away and got up slowly as Arsenio continued to mumble his confession. He backed toward the door and felt tentatively for the doorknob. When stung, Muhammad Ali danced to collect himself. Ben needed to do this now.

"Ben, Ben," said a voice from the hall. Ben opened the door and recognized George Marsh, the hospital's Dominican chaplain. Ordinarily, George would have administered the last rites, but Arsenio had insisted on a Filipino priest.

"You OK, Ben?" George asked as he peered into the room. Ben nodded.

"The doc wants back in; same with the cops."

"Sure you're OK?" he asked again.

Ben nodded again, lying.

"He doesn't have long—five minutes. OK?" George closed the door.

Ben breathed deeply. "OK," he whispered to himself and walked toward the bed. "OK."

Johnny was waiting as Ben walked down the hallway toward the hospital exit. He was smiling.

"Hey, Padre. You just made Arsenio a very happy Filipino," Johnny said as Ben approached. "Today he's goin' to heaven and gettin' a payback at the same time."

Ben didn't smile. "Swell," he said brusquely, walking close-mouthed with Johnny toward the door. He paused and turned toward the men's room. He felt a desperate need to wash.

You look like shit," Teddy loudly proclaimed, entering the cramped rectory kitchen. Ben was seated at a table, his hair uncombed, chin resting on the palm of his right hand. Nearby was his coffee mug, full of coffee long since dead, but Ben paid it and Teddy no mind.

Undeterred, Teddy walked toward the old tin coffee pot on the stove, all the while eyeing Ben intently, like he was the world's last barbecue rib. It was more than a month since Ben had returned from Manila, and over a week since Arsenio had been buried, but Ben seemed to be sinking into a deeper and bluer funk.

Teddy was worried. "Hey, Angelo," he said. "Man, lighten up." He opened the refrigerator door and looked inside for some cream. "There's just some stuff you can't help."

Teddy paused and stared at Ben to see if his words had any effect. They didn't. Clearly, more was needed.

Teddy sighed. "OK, man, you win."

He then walked toward the table and pulled from his pocket a pair of bright orange tickets, placing them beside Ben's cup of cold coffee. The tickets caught Ben's attention; they were for tonight's boxing card at the Georgetown Gym.

Teddy pointed at the tickets. "These here allow entry for two to an evening of pugilistic entertainment. They got some belligerent black folk gonna beat piss outa' each other for money and glory."

Teddy looked at Ben before continuing. "I was fixin' to ask this little cream-colored sister I been seein'. You know the one—high butt, straight nose, skinny legs. Works down at . . . "

Ben nodded that he did.

"She's sweet," Teddy rhapsodized. "Sweet," he added for emphasis, stretching the "eet." "But instead, Brother Angelo, I'll ask you.

"Come on, man. Smile." Teddy said. "Ain't gonna break your face."

Ben looked up at Teddy and chuckled. "It's OK, Teddy," he said softly. "I'll be OK. You don't always have to bail me out."

"Got to, *compadre*," Teddy said firmly. "Besides, you got a cuter ass."

The Georgetown Gym, a shabby relic from the city's blue-collar past. It was once a restaurant, now converted, sitting among a row of warehouses on the southern edge of downtown, seating capacity 400. That night it was maybe half-filled at best.

As Ben scanned the program, a single-sheet mimeo on cheap, coarse paper, he wondered if the fighters would get paid.

The preliminaries soon started and moved quickly along, the local prospects disposing of their hand-picked, out-of-town foes in first- or second-round KOs. The bouts, though artless and brutal, were predictable, a bit like wrestling, but the crowd—what crowd there was—loved it anyway.

During the last prelim, one young Mexican did little more than absorb blows for half a round before collapsing in his corner. The fluorescent ring light struck his pain-etched face, giving him a slightly Asian appearance as he lay, mouth open and eyes closed, writhing on the canvas.

Teddy was unsympathetic. "Look like some Vietnamese refugee," Teddy said derisively, pointing to the slender form of the fallen fighter. "Didn't know they had a boxing team."

Ben ignored him. Vietnam followed Teddy like a rain cloud on a string; he didn't like the Vietnamese and was horrified to learn there were refugee parishioners in St. Mary's. Ben had warned Teddy about his attitude. For the most part, Teddy bit his lip and complied. But away from St. Mary's was another matter. This time the comments slid by, and the lip bitten was Ben's.

Eventually, the beaten fighter was dragged from the ring by his handlers, all identically dressed in short gold jackets, the kid's name and hometown inscribed on their backs: "Lupe Mendoza, Sunnyside, WA." One of the handlers, an older man who resembled Lupe, was screaming at his charge, cursing him in equal parts English and Spanish. Lupe ignored him. At that moment, he had more pressing concerns, like placing one foot slowly in front of the other.

Teddy quickly stood up. He was indignant. His sympathy had shifted to the boy he'd just disparaged.

"Look at that jerk," he spat, nudging Ben. "Probably his old man. Fuckin' boxer wanna be. Overmatch his boy and expect somethin' more."

Lupe and his entourage walked down the aisle toward them. The man was still livid and continued loudly to badger his boy. It was more than Teddy could take. "*Papá, tú tienes la culpa!*

Estúpido!" Teddy shouted angrily, pointing his right index finger at the older man, who looked up, surprised. For a moment, it seemed he might respond, and Ben, who knew his friend well, hoped he wouldn't. He knew what *that* would trigger.

"Shit," he whispered, as he pulled on Teddy's forearm. It was taut and ready, and he didn't have to look to know the fist was clenched. Apparently, the old handler sensed the same thing, knowing in a heartbeat all that he needed to. He turned away and said nothing.

To Ben's relief, Teddy sat down. "Fuckin' chickenshit," he said angrily. "Never took a lick in his life. Fuckhead probably sells used cars to wetbacks."

"It's OK, man," Ben said soothingly, "it's OK. Relax, man. Another bout's coming up." Ben could see his efforts went nowhere. Teddy had folded his arms across his chest. He said nothing but his anger, volatile and simmering, was still obvious, still dangerous, and it made Ben nervous. He decided to change his approach.

He continued talking. "Man, you got a vent or somethin'?"

"What?"

"Eyes gettin' tight? There's steam from your ears, brother," Ben said evenly. "Wanna firetruck?" Teddy started to smile and Ben, on a roll, decided not to stop. "How 'bout an aid car? A taxi?" Ben paused. "Call Chinatown, getcha' rickshaw!"

Ben was doing Teddy. Turnabout was fair play and he knew the monologue by heart, complete with inflection and vocabulary. The patter had its desired effect, and his friend started to relax, dropping his arms from his chest.

Ben wasn't finished yet. His coup de grâce was next. "Come on, man," Ben said with just the proper Teddy-like concern, "Smile. It ain't gonna break your face."

Teddy recognized one of his signature comments. Ben was

right; the grin he couldn't prevent didn't break his face. "Got it down, brother."

"I should," Ben replied. "I've heard it enough."

Teddy slouched comfortably in his chair, tension drained. He looked calm and happy as he fished in his pocket for a cigarette. "Who's up?" he asked casually.

"Waterbug," Ben answered, referring to Wilbert "Waterbug" Anderson, whose thin build, quick hands, skittish style, and inappropriate first name gave birth to a more appropriate pugilistic sobriquet.

"He's still fightin'?" Teddy said, surprised. "I knew him when he started at the Boys Club. Fast hands, I'll give'm that. Problem is he hit like his name.

"Cockroach hit harder," he added derisively.

Teddy was back to normal, and Ben could now relax. He looked at his friend and wondered at how little he had changed. Teddy's world, part of which was once Ben's, was still black-and-white. Solutions were simple, direct, and sometimes violent.

Ben remembered those shared years with ambivalent fondness. He liked the simplicity, but he now hated and feared the violence. Boxing didn't count; it was a blood sport, but at least there were limits. People were seldom killed. The same couldn't be said of the murderous cycle now underway, triggered by Artie Del Rosario's death.

Ben wondered how many more would die before the killing would run its course. He feared the worst. He knew how Filipinos could nurture hatred, black and seemingly eternal, treating it like a pet sore to be scratched routinely to keep it from healing. Teddy was like that, and Ben was afraid that, at his own deepest core, he was too.

"Put out the smoke, asshole!" the voice, loud and angry,

came directly from behind where Teddy and Ben were sitting. Both turned toward the source, a large, bearded white man wearing a Cubs baseball cap.

"Who's askin'?" Teddy said, as he turned to look.

Ben resumed his calming litany. "It's OK, man," Ben whispered to his friend. "It's OK."

"I am," the man bellowed, and stood up. Ben studied him closely. He was big, maybe six-four and 230 pounds, most of it good weight. Ben was sure the fellow was confident nothing would happen, his size alone having deterred opponents in the past.

Teddy watched him as well, then slowly stood up. He was smaller by half a head and at least fifty pounds. Teddy stared at him and said nothing. The cigarette, halfway gone, dangled from between his right index and forefinger.

"Say 'please,' white boy," he said, in what sounded to Ben like a low, barely audible growl.

"Fuck you, chink," the man yelled and took a step forward. He was stopped by Teddy, who also stepped forward, snapping his right fist in a straight line aimed up and at the big man's face.

Teddy turned his body into the blow, pivoting powerfully to and through the point of impact. Experience had taught him always to lock his elbow, to take away any give and remove any doubt. When thrown right—the adrenalin high and the timing precise—the punch was remorseless; it hit like the butt end of a two-by-four. Or at least that's how it used to be. Teddy was older now, and a bit less certain. For insurance, he had jammed the lit end of the cigarette between the knuckles of his right index and forefingers. It found its mark an eyeblink after launch.

The move was so quick, Ben didn't even see the punch, but he heard the sharp clap of bone hitting bone. He flinched and turned away, sure Teddy had killed him. He was actually relieved to hear the man crying in pain.

For a Filipino, Teddy's hands were unusually large and strong. The single punch, even without the cigarette, broke the man open, splitting the skin from his left eyebrow to his cheekbone. The big man clapped both hands over the wound, trying vainly to stanch the flow of blood now dripping from the side of his face.

Ben could see the man was defenseless, but Teddy's instincts were those of the pit. He had one foot on a chair, ready to leap over and finish the job. Ben grabbed Teddy hard. "It's over, man," he said angrily. "Let's get the fuck outa' here."

Outside the Georgetown, Teddy and Ben walked toward the car. Teddy's adrenalin was still pumping, and his body shook as he spoke.

"Man, did you check that?" he said. "Did you check that?" he repeated, this time much louder.

Ben looked at him, but said nothing.

"Ain't lost a thing!" he yelled as he thrust his right fist skyward. "Not a goddamn thing!"

Ben stopped walking and looked at Teddy. "You could have put his eye out," he said quietly

"So what?" Teddy said. "Motherfucker deserved it and more. That 'C' on his cap should've been 'CS' for 'Cock Sucker.'"

Ben sighed. "Should've walked away, man."

Teddy was puzzled by his friend's attitude. "What's with you, man? That's how we handle things, or did you forget?"

"Did you forget?" Ben shot back angrily. Ben paused and looked away, trying hard to collect and control his words and thoughts. "Teddy, look at me, man," he said firmly, "I'm a priest. There's got to be a better way."

It was Saturday afternoon, and Ben walked from the rectory to the church. It was almost one o'clock, and confessions started on the hour. He felt good, like the normal rhythm of parish life was finally starting to return. That morning at coffee, Ben had apologized for the fight at the Georgetown, and evidently his sorrow was sincere. To test him, Ben casually mentioned he was baptizing a Vietnamese couple's firstborn infants at eleven—twins, he said. Teddy grimaced, but held his tongue. Ben hoped the change was permanent.

He entered the church and genuflected before walking to the confessional box at the rear. Of the seven sacraments, penance had become his favorite. It seemed to him the most human, particularly after Manila.

It was a funny switch. As a child, he had feared it most—the Saturday ritual in an ominous narrow box. He thought of it as an upright coffin, dark and narrow. There he whispered his sins, and absolution was granted, sometimes grudgingly.

Priests were different then. Taciturn and solemn, they seemed to be from the "you're sliding down a greased pole to hell and there's no way to stop it" school of theological thought, or so it once seemed to Ben. Still, he went each Saturday, despite powerful waves of apprehension which started to build on Thursday afternoon.

His world then was powered by a profound sense of fear and guilt, and though he dreaded confessions, the alternative of dying unclean frightened him even more.

In those years, Jesus did not have a human face. Or if He did, Ben was sure it was that of Big Daddy Lipscomb, the massive, spooky tackle for the Baltimore Colts. Each night after prayers, Ben took his plastic crucifix, kissing Big Daddy's wounds before clutching the cross to his chest. This gave protection against the night and sudden death. Nonetheless, one morning Ben almost died of fright when he rolled over and broke off one of the pierced, plastic hands.

But that was another time and, quite literally, another church. Talk of hell was now seldom heard, and God's love, rather than His retribution, was the staple of the day. In general, Ben welcomed the change. Religion shouldn't be the product of fear. But he still wondered on occasion if he would have chosen the priesthood without it.

It was an afternoon in May. Ben had been in the confessional for an hour. As usual, there were few serious sins or transgressions. He knew most of those who confessed, at least he knew their voices. He had learned early on that, sadly enough, those most in need of absolution seldom asked for it, at least not from him.

Time was passing quickly. There was nothing he hadn't heard before, nothing that shocked or challenged him. The Saturday regulars were there; the young boy—Ben guessed he was maybe twelve—who was driven by the same incomprehensible sense of guilt that had once overwhelmed Ben. He routinely confessed to impure thoughts. In his own defense, he said he shook his head hard whenever such thoughts came, trying physically to purge them from his mind. He had recently graduated to masturbation.

Then there was the old black woman who admitted to outbreaks of anger and occasional shoplifting. She wanted to talk forever, and Ben guessed she was more lonely than sinful. He wondered if the errors she confessed to were real, but he gave her his time and attention anyway.

"Father Ben," she would say as she finished, "you a nice man. I'll see you next week." And she would.

After she left, Ben glanced at his watch; it was two o'clock, and he stood up to leave. He was stopped by the familiar sounds of a door opening and a person dropping quietly to kneel. One more, Ben thought, as he slid the panel cover to hear this last Saturday confession.

"Bless me, Padre," said a voice Ben didn't recognize and could barely hear. It was a young, male, and heavily Filipino.

The boy was anxious, mumbling, mixing English words with what Ben recognized as Tagalog phrases. Finally, the tumbled monologue was entirely in the latter.

"Pardon," Ben interrupted him. "In English, please." Ben was uncomfortable in these situations; it made him feel patronizing. He had been on the receiving end often enough himself in the past. It was what he had wanted to tell the archbishop about, but didn't.

The voice on the other side of the black screen partition seemed terribly confused. "I, I thought you was Pilipino," he said clearly, his accent substituting a "P" for an "F."

"I am," Ben said, then paused before adding in Cebuano, *"Pero natawo 'ko sa Amerika."* It meant he was U.S.-born and raised. He hoped the boy would understand but doubted it. From Remedios, he learned that speakers of Tagalog, the national language, rarely bothered with other dialects.

"But, but. . . " the boy stammered.

"Please, son," Ben interrupted. "I don't speak Tagalog."

The boy sighed. "Padre, I. . . " he whispered.

"Yes," Ben said as he moved his ear closer to the mesh screen.

"Never mind," he said quietly. "Never mind."

There was nothing else, just the sound of quiet movement, and a door opening, then slowly closing.

Ben was sitting in the cramped rectory kitchen, his feet perched atop a small, wooden table. It was two-thirty,

Saturday afternoon, and the house, for a change, was deserted. He sipped slowly on a cold Budweiser, intending to nurse it as long as possible. Outside he could see two young boys in the church parking lot playing basketball, much as he had done two decades before.

For the inner city, outdoor hoops were a surer sign of spring than baseball, which had long ago lost its lure for the boys of St. Mary's. It was no wonder, Ben thought. Basketball was fast, aggressive, and muscularly graceful—a sport in which the ego is supreme. The game's requisites were a perfect match for kids who possessed, or thought they possessed, such traits.

Though the window was closed, he could hear bits of their banter punctuated by the dribble of a nylon ball hard against concrete. It was the eternal debate of youth. Who's the best? The baddest? Magic or Bird?

In his own day, it was West or Oscar. A sweet continuity—Ben was pleased.

Perhaps a more normal life was now returning, and the bounce of a ball was its herald. He couldn't be sure, but he hoped it would, and soon. All he wanted, he told Teddy that morning over coffee, was a funeral where the deceased wasn't a victim. Old age, a car accident, cancer—anything, he said, was better than the *barkada* cycle.

He thought briefly about the young Filipino's aborted confession. It bothered him a bit, but he dismissed it quickly. It had happened before, and would, he assumed, happen again. He resolved to tell the archbishop; it might mean a transfer from St. Mary's, maybe to a white parish up north. It was a choice he wouldn't fight. But that was for later, after a gathering of nerve.

For now, he looked forward to the rest of the day and night. Unlike most Saturdays, nothing was scheduled. He might, he thought, just stay home and read, or shop a bookstore in the

University District, or catch a movie. Or better yet, he could grab a bite and drive to Lake Washington, sit on a dock, and watch old men fish for perch and trout.

The choice was easy: a quick burger, then a drive to the lake. Clara was right about aesthetics; it wasn't just for the rich.

He gulped what was left of the Bud and hurried out of the kitchen. It was spring and, in Seattle, the bright afternoon sun promised more than it could deliver. Ben rummaged through the hallway closet for a light nylon parka but settled instead for a heavier woolen coat. He knew it would be cold by the water, particularly as the afternoon light grew dimmer.

A book, he thought, might be nice. He started toward his room, but quickly changed his mind and turned on his heel toward the door. He just wanted to enjoy the lake without distraction, literary or otherwise. Besides, the longer he tarried, the more likely it was that his services would be summoned.

Outside was his old blue Datsun, the quintessential beater. Its muffler was corroded and fastened to the chassis by a piece of bent coat hanger. Recently, each time he drove it, parts would fall off. First, there was the outside rear-view mirror, then a hubcap. The last time out, it was part of the exhaust pipe. There was no effort at replacement, Ben thinking that this process of incremental stripping—the automotive equal of death by slicing—was a sign of the end. He only hoped there were a few miles left.

Ben rarely drove his car now, preferring the plush appointments of the red Cadillac. Teddy had nicknamed the Datsun "Janis," after Janis Joplin, not because he liked her singing, which passed for music, but because of its many miles of hard, unforgiving road.

On the way out the door, Ben greeted the mailman who was walking toward the rectory. He was tempted to stop and inspect the packet of letters, but didn't. It was, he figured, just bills or junk mail. These could wait. Nothing should interfere with this rare and lovely time, not bills or a book or anything that could detract from his aesthetic afternoon.

Between the beaches at Leschi and Seward Park in the city's south end, a solitary fishing dock extends for thirty yards or so into the lake. When they were kids, Ben and Teddy used to ride their bikes to it—a five-mile trip, much of it uphill from where they lived.

Within that distance, they passed several different worlds, starting with their own houses and ending with the posh lakefront mansions owned by thin, pink people. The pink people would stare at the boys as they passed; their looks grew more intense if the caravan included black riders.

Ben and Teddy noticed the surveillance, but being young, they shrugged it off. They proceeded to the dock where they'd fish, swim, or sip Cokes and do little else. In his childhood those were memories, fond and warm, and now he was returning.

The fishermen were there on the dock, huddled and silent in oversize jackets. Even as a kid, Ben knew they were serious men who fished rain, shine, and in-between. Their ritual was solemn and virtually wordless, seldom punctuated by human sound, save an occasional "gotta go."

Twenty years ago, most of those fishing were old black men, patient and dignified in the pursuit of their passion. Ben and Teddy felt comfortable and safe among them, sharing the serenity on this long, narrow dock. In deference, the boys would lower their voices, often lapsing into long, uncharacteristic periods of silence, more appropriate for early morning mass.

For Ben, as he walked down the dock, little had changed.

He chose a spot on the end and dangled his feet over the edge. As a boy he had done the same thing, but now the waves occasionally touched his shoe soles. He adjusted, pulling back just a bit. In the distance, he could see the Cascades, a stunning, snow-capped backdrop to a city that now was undergoing seasonal change.

So much had happened in the Philippines, perhaps too much for him to fully understand. So he had shut out the days in Manila, treating them like some kind of aberration. And perhaps they were. But in the closing of that door, abrupt and sure, maybe he had missed something, like why it was open in the first place.

For the first time since mailing his letter to Ellen, Ben thought hard about her, and sorrow coursed straight to his heart. The wind had started to whip, driving the old men deeper into their coats. The wind or sorrow, or both, he wasn't sure, brought stinging tears to Ben's eyes.

The water was getting rougher. One by one, the fishermen reeled in their lines, packed their gear and left.

"Gotta go," he heard them say. "Gotta go."

Finally, only Ben was left, surrounded by darkening beauty. He didn't notice. His thoughts were elsewhere, in a city where beauty had vanished, and with a woman whose beauty had not.

When Ben returned, the rectory was dark. Teddy wasn't home, not unusual on a Saturday night. He had found a new woman, Sugar Silverio, a pretty *mestiza* whose parents lived in the parish. Sugar, Ben thought, was an odd choice. She was a recently divorced mother of three, and her ex-husband still haunted her, threatening to kill his successor. The ex was, by all accounts, a violent and spooky man with bullet fragments embedded deep in his thick skull. The situation would have discouraged most potential suitors, but not Teddy.

"She got points, Angelo," he explained, "firm, high points."

For Teddy that was enough. Nevertheless, every time he went over to Sugar's, he carried his argument—a .45-caliber semi-automatic—on his right hip.

Ben worried about the situation and its potential for violence, but Teddy reassured him. "I'm a slave to love," he said lightly. "But don't worry, Brother Angelo, in the event of unreasonableness, I pitch, he catches.

"And besides," he added, "I got silver bullets."

Ben parked the Datsun in front of the church under a bright street light and quickly checked the sidewalk both ways before leaving his car. Old habits, he thought.

Inside the rectory, he turned on the light. The afternoon mail sat on a flower stand in the hallway. Someone, probably Teddy, had put it there. He grabbed the small bundle and headed to his room.

Ben sat at his desk, quickly sorting the mail. Most of it was junk. There were a couple of bills, which he laid neatly to the side to be opened tomorrow. In his haste, he almost missed the thin blue envelope lodged between the pages of a color catalogue for women's summer wear.

For a moment, his heart seemed to stop. He knew it was from the Philippines, even before he saw the multicolored "Pilipinas" stamps. It had to come—Ellen's response. Thousands of miles was not enough distance or protection for protests from the heart.

He placed the letter in the center of his desk and leaned back in his chair, staring for a moment at the ceiling. He tried to imagine what razor-tipped arrows the blue envelope might contain.

Ben breathed deeply, pulled himself forward, and inspected

the letter closely. He immediately recognized the handwriting and return address. The sender was Clara, not Ellen, and he was relieved. Although Ben thought there might be a reprimand, it would be mild, like a parental scolding, and far easier to take.

Almost eagerly, he broke the seal, pulling out a four-page letter written on onion-skin paper. Clara's script was tiny, intricate, and unreadable by the light of the small desk lamp. Slowly, he stood up and walked to the switch on the wall. He blinked his eyes hard, adjusting to the more powerful light, and returned to his desk.

Through the first three pages, his aunt was chatty and casual. She hoped he had enjoyed himself and would return soon. She also apologized for her absence, citing the need for her presence elsewhere. "Business reasons," she explained obliquely. Clara then mentioned the recent political disturbances in Manila, blaming Communists and "other anti-government agitators," before adding that order would "soon be restored."

For the first three pages, Clara said nothing of Ellen, and for that he was surprised but glad. Ben was never able to fathom the extent or nature of their relationship. He had seen them together just once, at dinner at his aunt's, and neither before nor after had either said much about the other.

Was Ellen just an employee or something more? He didn't know, but he hoped it was the former, which would make mention of Ellen, or Aunt Clara's advocacy of her cause, much less likely.

Ben turned the page and stared blankly at the first paragraph. Dread and a feeling of numbness overwhelmed him. Ellen was dead. She was killed in a "terrible accident" which Clara did not describe. "Anyway, Ellen was a good and trusted assistant, and I will miss her dearly. As you well know, I do not pray, but it is appropriate for you to do so."

That was it, a few sentences summing up the end of a life. Nothing more.

Ben folded the letter neatly along the creases and put it back in the envelope. He was like a man on a narrow ledge, bound to fall. The only question was when.

Control, he told himself, control. He had to have it, at least for a while, because he feared the alternative. He was afraid of letting go and of realizing, at some point in the process, what he had lost.

Ben pushed down hard on the arms of the chair. He wanted to stand, but when he did, he swayed drunkenly, his legs suddenly gelatinous. His bed was just a few feet away and his only thought was of reaching it. Control, he said again, control.

Like a child learning to walk, he stood, then moved, trying to impose his will on muscles that seemed now to respond to other masters. One more step, he thought, just one more step.

Finally, he was there. He fell forward like a loaded sack onto the mattress. He bounced once, then a second time, then not at all. With great effort, he turned his body to lie on his back, feeling a tremor in his legs and a weakness throughout. This, he thought, must be what hell is like, the loss of hope.

He could see the clock on his desk; it was almost eleven and sleep was out of the question. His fate was to lie there alone, thinking of Ellen and of words not said. He wasn't sure he could make it through to that magical cup of morning coffee. Funny, he thought, that's how he typically advised despondent members of his flock. "Just make it to the morning, to that fresh cup of coffee." His words mocked him now; he was uncertain the good doctor could heal himself.

The telephone at the edge of his bed was perhaps his only chance of salvation. Ben reached for it with strength he wasn't sure was there. He closed his eyes, trying hard to see numbers which, under ordinary circumstances, he knew by heart. It was late, but he didn't care. People called him regardless of the hour, and tonight, the favor must be returned.

Night moves. Teddy and Sugar lay naked, intertwined on a bed. They were breathing heavily, but were otherwise silent and still. In the room hung the heavy scent of passion, thick and moist, upon which air from an open window made no impression.

"Smell like fuckin' to me," Teddy whispered. "Sweet."

"Yourself," she said, as she moved her hand between his legs. "I want it again."

Teddy smiled. "You know Filipinos," he said. "We're a friendly people."

"Good," she purred, as she mounted him, biting and licking his neck. She paused there, just a rest stop on the trip south. Like a Toro mower, she would cover every inch.

Teddy was ecstatic. "This is better than Debra Winger doin' Richard Gere in *An Officer...* "

Sugar interrupted him. "Better, baby," she said.

"Damn near slid off the screen," he said between gasps.

Film critics in love, or at least in heat—but near the height, the telephone rang.

"Damn!" they both said together as Sugar reached for the phone and Teddy swung to the other side. He picked up the .45 and brought it to the bed. He then inspected the gun and unlocked the safety.

"Fuckin' asshole," he said.

"It's for you, baby," Sugar said, handing him the receiver. She then reclined against the headboard.

As Teddy listened, he was silent, concern etching his face. "Be right there, Angelo," he finally said before hanging up.

He turned toward Sugar, who made no effort to hide her disappointment. "Baby," he said, "I gotta... "

His sentence was cut short by her hand, reinserted between his legs.

"Baby," he said weakly. "Me and Angelo, we're *compadres.*"

Sugar was atop him now, this time lower on his trunk.

"Fuck it," he said as he spread his legs. "Half an hour ain't gonna kill him."

Nah," Teddy said as Ben started to tell his Manila tale. Earlier, he had found his friend in his room. He was lying on his bed, flat on his back and covered with sweat. His body was shaking. Quickly, Teddy wetted a hand towel, pressing it firmly against Ben's face and chest. He then lifted him to his feet, wrapping Ben's arm around his neck, and walked him to the kitchen.

"You a motherfuckin' mess, man," he said. He sat Ben down on a kitchen chair and went straight to the refrigerator, where the coffee container was stored.

"Leave you alone," he said, as he filled the coffee pot with water, "and you fuckin' fall apart."

At that time, he had no idea what ailed his friend, but for Teddy, coffee and cigarettes were universal antidotes. They cured colds, viruses, hangovers, and breaks of the heart. Doctor Teddy's prescription, primitive though it was, had an immediate and positive effect. Ben became more relaxed and animated, sitting at the table, both hands curled around a hot cup of fresh black coffee.

As Ben continued his story, Teddy stared at him in disbelief.

"Nah," he said again, shaking his head at the picture being

painted. Eventually, Ben finished by describing what Aunt Clara had written in the letter. He looked at Teddy for a reaction and, for a while, there was none.

"So, what's the point, man?" Teddy finally said. "This lady you had a thing with dies. It was sweet while it lasted, and now it's over. But that's life, brother."

Ben was surprised by Teddy's comments. Expecting sympathy, at least a bit, he got far less.

"OK, OK," Teddy said. "Don't get pissed. Maybe I'm too hard. You sorry she's gone and all, and it's cool to mourn the dead. But her being gone ain't your fault."

Teddy paused before going on. "It just ain't your fault," he repeated, this time with much greater force. "I know you, Angelo, remember? We grew up together. You blame yourself for everything. Remember? When Pope Pius died you wanted to confess that. Remember? Motherfucker died on his own. Same with Ellen, man. Don't hang this on yourself."

Teddy stopped for a moment to assess his friend. "Look man," he said in a softer voice and with a slower cadence. His words were carefully chosen, "It's your first time. I know that. And maybe you thought there was somethin' there. Somethin' workable."

Teddy looked at Ben. Although still silent, Ben shrugged in reply.

"Face it, Angelo," he said bluntly "If there was somethin' there, I mean somethin' really sweet, no way you would've come back, man. I mean no way. And that's the truth."

Maybe Teddy was right; his words haunted Ben for days, starting in the shadows of his mind and gradually growing in prominence. Through it all, Teddy stayed close by, always ready to reinforce his message, usually by providing irrefutable examples from the past. Ben needed the hectoring, prone as he was to guilt and self-pity. Teddy understood this.

On one such occasion in midweek, Teddy caught his friend at coffee and recalled for him the story of "Zorro," whose real name had been Carmen Gamboa. Carmen was a young, pretty Mexican girl from eastern Washington, a newcomer to their eighth-grade class. Her only blemish was a moderate amount of facial hair.

Adolescent humor is often cruel, and poor Carmen, being new, was its designated victim. Teddy coined the nickname on her second day, combining her ethnic heritage with the unfortunate trace of a mustache. The nickname, as is often the case, stuck, and she carried it with her, though not without protest.

Carmen was continually fighting. Once she struck Teddy from behind as he walked down the hall. Though stunned and angry, he just stared. "Get a shave, bitch," he finally said, before turning and walking away. "Zorro" survived that occasion, but eventually, the harrassment proved to be too much. She transferred to another school after Christmas, and was seldom heard from.

B en had been the only eighth-grader to befriend Carmen, and he was careful to address her by her Christian name. She was touched by his kindness, an infatuation amplified by her otherwise hostile environment. She would do things to catch Ben's eye, and she waited for chances to speak to him alone.

A t first, when they were together, they would talk about anything, it seemed. Carmen soon learned that Ben's passion was professional basketball and, although unfamiliar with the topic when she started school in September she was soon spouting statistics and giving player evaluations like a veteran hoop junkie.

She once told Ben that Oscar was better than West because he was more versatile. To Ben, the statement was heresy, but he admired her knowledge nevertheless.

Although he liked Carmen, he never led her on, or so he thought. He knew that in a few short months, his destination was the seminary. Talk of "boyfriend and girlfriend," or "going steady" was simply out of the question. Carmen knew, or Ben thought she did, that this was understood.

And of course it was, from Ben's resolute perspective. It came, therefore, as a shock when he discovered that in this life there can be more than one opinion.

It happened one cold, dry December afternoon. Class was out, and Ben and Carmen were walking together. Christmas was coming, but Ben was already thinking about the NBA finals the following spring. He was full of hope and argued that his beloved Lakers would finally upset the Celtics, the perennial league kingpins.

"Russell's old," he said bluntly, referring to the great Celtic center. "He's had it, and besides, no one can shut out West and Baylor forever." Ben's voice was firm and full of thirteen-year-old resolve.

It turned out he was wrong on all counts, basketball and otherwise. Carmen, instead of responding as she usually did to his obvious invitation to debate the sport's probabilities, simply let the comment pass.

Ben, a bit surprised, continued nevertheless. "It's West," he said loudly, mimicking an announcer describing the smooth, quick moves of the great Laker guard, "taking the feed from Ellis. There's ten seconds left in regulation, score knotted at 92–all. West dribbles to the top of the key. Jones is on him tight. He stops! He shoots! It's good! Lakers win!"

The victory sealed, Ben collapsed on the lawn. "It was nothin', guys," he murmured, as imaginary teammates surged forward to congratulate him. Carmen wasn't among them; basketball wasn't on her agenda. Instead, she hung back, biting her lip and wrinkling her nose. She was trying to build up nerve, and the effort showed on her thirteen-year-old face.

Ben was oblivious, a trait not uncommon among boys, young or old. "That's how it's gonna be, Carmen," he said happily, as he lay on the lawn, gazing up at the blue afternoon sky. In his mind, he saw waves of speedy Lakers breaking by Celtics for easy scores.

Carmen wished his gaze and his thoughts were on her, but Ben's monologue continued. "I mean this spring we can watch the finals and, believe me, it'll happen just like that, just like I said." He sat up abruptly and looked at her. Carmen now had one of her wishes. "I mean," Ben said, "I'd like to watch it with you because..." He hesitated at that point, looking for the right word. "You know what I mean," he said finally, putting the burden of definition temporarily on Carmen. "We've become *friends*—you know, *buddies*."

Terms meant to endear and comfort, in the hands of a novice, are deadly. Carmen was crushed. Without a word, she turned on her heel, carrying herself with the arrogant grace of a flamenco dancer. She avoided Ben after that, and when school resumed in January, Carmen Gamboa wasn't there.

Then, as now, Teddy laid it all out, and what he said had been obvious to everyone but Ben. Ben was surprised that, in Teddy's opinion, Carmen was in love with him. "Could've got you some," Teddy said with his usual lack of tact. "I mean, she got a mustache and all, but shit."

Ben was astonished by his friend's revelation. "I didn't know, Muhammad," he said. "I just didn't."

Teddy looked hard at his friend. "Maybe it's good you entering the seminary, Angelo," he said with a trace of sarcasm. "Cuz if you gonna make it, you gonna need a boatload of God's grace."

It was Teddy, too, who periodically kept him current on Carmen. He had friends at her new school, and the news he brought was disturbing. She'd fallen in with an older, faster crowd, many of whom weren't even students. They often drank and were rowdy at parties and public functions.

One report placed Carmen in Volunteer Park late at night. She was in the back seat of a '56 Ford and her partner was an eighteen-year-old bound for the army. It was clear basketball wasn't a major topic of conversation.

When Ben heard this, he walked over to her house. He just wanted to talk to her, but she wouldn't even come to the door. As he left the porch, he looked back and saw Carmen peeking through an opening in the drapes which quickly closed. It was the last time he saw her.

Two weeks later she was dead, killed in a high-speed crash on Highway 99 which also claimed her soldier-to-be. They had rear-ended a low riding Chev pickup that was carrying fifteen-foot sections of thick steel pipe. The sections extended several feet beyond the edge of the truck's bed, a red warning flag affixed to the end of one of the pipes. Carmen was behind the steering wheel of the Ford, crushed against its rigid column. She was drunk at the time, and her severed head was found sitting beside a six-pack of Bud in the back seat.

That was it for Carmen Gamboa, but not for Ben. He attended the closed-casket funeral and cried in the rear of the church. His tears did not stop with the end of the ceremony, and Carmen's memory—more specifically a pervasive feeling that her death was somehow his fault—stalked him like a nocturnal predator.

His parents tried talking to him. Remedios tried in particular, but she was in no position to do so. He was her son much more than his father's, and he had inherited her intense religiosity, from the day he was first able to distinguish demons from angels, and salvation from hell.

It took Teddy to set Ben straight. "Listen, fool," he was constantly urging. "Bitch's fault, not yours." One afternoon Teddy visited Ben at his home. He came armed with extensive background material on the deceased, and he quickly launched into his morose friend. The point of this latest harangue was that Carmen was bound to live hard and die fast anyway. One of his buddies at her new school, Curtis, had said as much. Curtis had come to know Carmen real well, and she confided in him. Now those secrets were there for Ben to review posthumously.

According to Curtis, Carmen was an abused child and didn't even know her real dad. "The man at her house was her stepfather," Teddy said, "and you know what assholes those guys are." He winked lasciviously. "Her mom and stepdad are drunks," he added, "and if you thought you had June and Ward, brother, better think again. She came here 'cuz no school over there'd take her. Fuckin' and fightin', man, and born to lose."

For the first time in several days, Ben was listening. Teddy, sensing this, went for it. "She killed her own self, Angelo," he said slowly, "and all you did, man I mean *all* you did, was postpone the day."

It all came back to Ben. Like water stored from winters past then suddenly released, it touched all parts. Images, once distant and faded, were suddenly fresh and very painful.

He winced at the memories. As Teddy closed the story of "Zorro," Ben was subdued, but, for the first time in several days, he felt a tinge of relief. Teddy stared at him with a manic, relentless intensity, as if by so doing, the healing would start. Maybe, thought Ben, it wasn't my fault, Ellen's death. There appeared the start of a smile.

Teddy noticed it even before Ben. "Later, man," he said, his job done as he rose from the kitchen table. "Me and Sugar's got business."

Ben looked up. "Thanks," he said, as his friend headed toward the door.

Teddy paused and turned toward him. "Yo' mama's gone, Angelo," he said slowly. "But there's still me."

Ben nodded and looked at the clock as Teddy walked out the rectory door. It was almost noon, and several hours had passed without notice. He stood and grabbed the half-filled cups of coffee, bringing them to the sink.

Already he felt better, much lighter. There were duties to attend to and errands to run. Outside, though the window was closed, he could hear the bounce of a nylon basketball hard against concrete.

— 9 —

Payback

So after all these years, poor Carmen Gamboa did a good turn—and no strings attached. Teddy's story of Zorro was the perfect cure. Although Ben's sorrow remained, his sense of guilt was ebbing. With added fervor, he immersed himself in his priestly and parish duties, almost forgetting for a while his deeply felt loss.

A week or so later, he could see Teddy pacing nervously outside of his rectory office. Ben was counseling a young couple intending to marry, apprising them of the solemnity of that pact they were about to enter.

Teddy peered inside the partly open door. He was speaking silently to Ben, mouthing his words in slow, exaggerated fashion.

Ben looked up, irritated. "Cut this shit," Teddy was saying. Ben gave him his sternest look and went back to the matter at hand.

Teddy persisted. He motioned vigorously for his friend to

come out and Ben, seeing his determination, stood up and excused himself. As he entered the hallway, closing the door quietly behind him, he could tell by his friend's face and demeanor that he wasn't playing. Something serious was up.

"Sorry, man," Teddy said apologetically, "I'da never... "

Ben interrupted him. "It's OK, man," he said.

"There's big trouble," he said. "I mean serious shit."

"What?"

"I just got back from Chinatown," Teddy said, trying hard to keep his voice from rising. "Sittin' in a booth in the New Hong Kong and I heard these dudes talkin', man. Hard-talkin', Neanderthal FOBs, but not from here. Never seen 'em."

The words came in a rush, and Teddy stopped to catch his breath before starting again. "Anyway, man, they were talkin' Ilocano, real hush-hush. In a Chinese joint, no Chinaman *comprende*. But I caught it, man. My mom's Ilocano."

By now, Ben was caught up in his friend's excitement. "Well, come on," he said impatiently.

"Hit, man," Teddy said. "Cats from outside. Stockton, maybe. Payback for Arsenio's killin', you know, where the mom and dad got it too."

Ben nodded. "Shit," he whispered.

"Hey," Teddy said, shrugging his shoulders. "It had to happen, man. You know how Filipinos are. It's goin' down."

"When?"

"Tonight, maybe sooner."

The drive to Cora Del Rosario's was eight minutes from the rectory and the powerful red Caddy covered it in half the time. Ben tried phoning ahead, but no one answered. Next, he tried the cops, but they were notably slow about crimes near St. Mary's. Anyway, a crime hadn't occurred, at least not yet.

About half a block from the house, Teddy turned off the engine, allowing the car to coast to a halt. They would approach cautiously and on foot. He had learned this trick the hard way, from a cop in California who caught him burglarizing a house.

Teddy put his index finger to his lips, signaling Ben to be silent. They got out of the car on opposite sides, taking care to close the doors quietly. They moved warily forward, from parked cars, to trees, to telephone poles, always behind or near cover. Nothing might have happened, but there was no sense in taking chances.

Near the gate of the high wooden fence surrounding the Del Rosario's front yard, Teddy motioned for his friend to stay crouched and on the sidewalk. Under no condition should Ben enter the yard. Teddy would survey the rear and sides of the house.

Ben obeyed, although he felt a bit foolish, particularly as drivers stopped to stare before going by. Still, he thought, better foolish than dead.

Teddy was gone maybe five minutes, and when he returned he was smiling and relaxed. "No sign of entry," he said. "Seems no one's home."

"Good," Ben said, relieved, as he stood and happily shook the kinks out of his lower back and legs. "What do we do now?"

"Wait for the cops," Teddy said. "Hey," he added, "I know they're slow, but they'll come sometime. We'll go sit in the car."

As they turned toward the Caddy, they heard a familiar voice from behind calling Ben's name. It was Cora Del Rosario, who was sitting on the passenger side of a late-model Chrysler driven by Eduardo, her middle son.

Eduardo was younger than Teddy and Ben, but both knew him well, at least by reputation. He was a tough, hot-tempered boy, constantly in and out of trouble. After the killing of Arsenio and his parents, he had been picked up as a suspect in the murders. However, his alibi held and he was free, at least for now.

Both Ben and Teddy were convinced Eduardo had something to do with the killings, and that only his cunning, which was considerable, had kept him free.

"Hello, Manang," Ben said warmly, as he walked toward the car to open Cora's door. As he drew nearer, he could see the back seat was full of grocery bags. "I'll help you with these later," he said, pointing to the bags. "But let's go inside first, I have something to... "

The sentence was stopped by a powerful jolt at waist level, hurling Ben forward and hard onto the concrete sidewalk. He bumped his forehead, and felt the sharp recoil of his neck. He knew he was losing consciousness, but not before he heard explosions nearby—three, maybe four—strong, but growing fainter, and what he thought was the death scream of Cora Del Rosario.

When Ben came to, Teddy's dark brown face was hovering in front of him like a huge carnivorous bird. But unlike any bird, he smelled of chow mein. On the bedside table stood take-out containers—all empty.

"I'da saved you some, man," Teddy began, "but I didn't know how long you'd be out. No sense wastin' good food, so I ate it."

"How long have I been out?" Ben asked groggily, trying hard to adjust his unfocused eyesight.

"A day," Teddy said. "You were a mess after I'd tackled you. Man, you gotta learn how to fall. Looked like one of them cartoon characters, you know, like Elmer Fudd."

Ben ignored the unflattering comparison. His eyesight was slowly improving, but still blurred. He touched his head, which throbbed like a small Cuban conga, and found it sore and heavily bandaged.

"You had a pretty bad concussion, man," Teddy explained, "plus they got some stitches in you.

"Never could take a punch," he added.

"What happened?"

"Hit, just like I said," Teddy explained calmly. "All's I saw was a window down and a short black barrel stickin' out. They were comin' from behind, so you didn't have a chance. Same with Cora and her boy. Caught the car and the plates, though. From California, like they said."

Ben didn't hear the first part. "Cora's. . . " he began, unable to continue.

"Than a doorknob, man," Teddy said, finishing the sentence. "Same with Eduardo. Chest and belly, twelve gauge. Both of 'em."

Ben wanted to scream, anything to purge his absolute revulsion. But his head hurt too much. Instead, he clenched his fists and repeatedly pounded them together in front of his chest.

"But that's life," Teddy said calmly. "And the most important thing's you ain't joined 'em. And besides, you know Filipinos. The cycle's completin' and all. It's goin' to the last man, and my advice is we just stay the fuck out the way."

Teddy stopped, interrupted by the sound of a door opening. He turned to look. The visitor was Johnny Romero, dressed in civilian clothes but carrying a pad and pen.

Teddy didn't like policemen, and, even out of uniform, Johnny still looked like a cop. That was fine with Johnny, who didn't like criminals, even reformed ones. He might have used his power to dog Teddy hard—there had been a number of chances since he returned from California—but somewhere in Johnny Romero's memory was an unhappy vision of Teddy beating him senseless when they were boys.

"Johnny's here," Teddy loudly announced. "Just like a cop, late as usual. He's gonna take your statement. I already told him you didn't see shit, but he's an ignorant, hard-headed motherfucker."

Teddy stared at Johnny, who stood near the foot of the bed. Neither man smiled.

"I'ma leave you now, Angelo," Teddy said abruptly as he turned toward the open door. "Just tell the man you didn't see nuthin', and I'll pick you up in three–four days."

"Three or four days!" Ben cried. The thought of staying in a hospital that long unnerved him.

"Observation, man," Teddy said as he closed the door. "You got a hole in your head, Angelo. You ain't Superman."

A week later Ben was finally released from the hospital. He went straight to the rectory. On the kitchen table a message was waiting; Aunt Clara had called earlier that afternoon.

Immediately he felt uneasy. Maybe his aunt would talk about Ellen. He quickly dismissed the thought, remembering her letter—Ellen's death had been only cursorily mentioned. In fact, Clara's purpose now was probably to chide him like a schoolboy.

It had been over two weeks since the letter from Manila had arrived at the rectory, which meant Clara had written it a week before that. Undoubtedly, he told himself, she was calling to scold him for not promptly responding. Ben had almost forgotten that that's how it had been when he was growing up—a tardy response on his part inevitably followed by a long-distance reprimand by telephone, sometimes from different parts of the world. Given his age, it seemed all a bit silly now, but that's how Clara was and how she would always be.

He walked to his room and picked up the phone, then dialed

the international operator. He gave her the number of Clara's home in Manila, which he knew by heart, and waited patiently for the connection. It was early Saturday evening in Seattle and Sunday midmorning in Manila. Although he couldn't remember the exact number of hours difference, the evening-morning dichotomy was easy enough to recall, and he had always used it as his rule of thumb. Clara, he thought, should be home. Unless guests were present, she rarely left the house before noon.

Early Saturday night wasn't a time for a sharp red Caddy with plush appointments to stay parked for long in front of an old Catholic church. An hour earlier, Teddy had picked up Ben at the hospital and deposited him at the front door of St. Mary's. Ben had suggested to his friend that he come in for a beer. The offer was declined. Couldn't, he said. Sugar was expecting him.

With that, he took off, wheels screeching, quick as a jet on a short runway. He soon arrived at Sugar's and inspected his gun and both sides of the street before leaving his car. He would have preferred another rendezvous, but screwing at the rectory was out of the question, even for Teddy.

Once inside her house, there was a perfunctory greeting— "Hey, Baby"—followed by a minute's worth of crotch-rubbing, tongue-sucking embraces. They were soon in the Cadillac and moving down the street for a Saturday night on the town.

That morning Sugar had checked the paper—the entertainment section, one of the few things she read—and decided on an action film. Teddy readily agreed. Their easy concurrence was no surprise. They'd been together a bit less than two months and in that time, their fare had seldom varied: a movie with lots of action and minimal dialogue, followed by beers and burgers and a quick trip home.

As Teddy drove, he had one hand on the wheel and the other lodged under Sugar's dress and between her legs. He was massaging the inside of her smooth, naked thighs and other parts as well. Sugar bit her lip and leaned back.

"I could scream," she whispered as she arched her back, pushing her shoulders hard against the car seat.

Teddy smiled. "Scream, Baby," he said. "Ain't no one but us gonna' hear. I'll even roll up the window."

Although Teddy was watching traffic, he could see Sugar out of the corner of his right eye, raising and lowering her body. She strained against the seat, and he felt her thighs growing warm as he stroked the crotch of her cotton panties, first on, then under the fabric. This auto-erotic activity changed their best-laid plans.

"Baby," Sugar said. "Let's skip the movie and go home. We'll catch it tomorrow."

They were maybe a mile away from the theater. Teddy smiled as he turned on the signal light near an intersection. He would turn here, figuring they'd be back at her place in less than ten minutes.

But first, there was the small matter of gas. Teddy noticed the tank was near empty, which wasn't unusual since it was never anywhere near full. For Teddy, it was the only drawback to the car; ten miles to the gallon at its very best. On his salary, a full tank, like sex at the rectory, was out of the question.

The most he would spend at the pump was five dollars, for regular, and that only after he had cruised a ten-mile radius looking for the lowest self-serve price. Sometimes, he'd spend as low as three, but would draw the line there; anything less— to power a mint-condition Cadillac—was embarrassing. Teddy quickly decided on the lower end of the range, counting out three bills from a money clip binding currency comprised entirely of ones.

"Be right back, Baby," he said as he opened the car door.

It was a pre-pay, self-serve, combination gas-and-Chinese-food-takeout station—cash only, no check or credit card. That was fine with Teddy, who had neither of the last two and little of the first.

Inside the brightly lit building that housed this odd combination of products, he waited patiently, the last customer in a short line to the counter. While waiting, he amused himself by mugging for the newly installed "Robber Proof" camera overhead.

The clerk, a young black man, was fast and efficient. Teddy had seen him before, but didn't like him much. He thought he was rude and sarcastic, maybe thinking this job was just a stopover on his way to some corporate top. Think again, fool, Teddy thought.

The customer just before Teddy was a ragged old Indian man. "That'll be two-twenty, Chief," the clerk said as he pushed the Indian's purchase—three single cigarettes and a bottle of cheap wine—quickly toward him. "No checks, OK?" he added.

The clerk's condescending tone irritated Teddy, and he could feel the muscles in the back of his neck start to tighten. The old man looked vainly in his pocket for loose change, and it quickly became clear he didn't have enough.

"Sorry, Chief," the clerk said as he pulled back the wine and cigarettes. "No credit, either."

For a moment, the Indian stared at his tormentor, as if he might say or do something. He didn't, though. He just turned and left.

"Next," the clerk said as he wiped the counter's surface with a rag. It was where the old man had placed his hands.

Teddy took a second to calm himself before stepping forward. Be cool, he told himself.

"Next," the clerk repeated.

"Yeah," Teddy began. "Uh, three dollars regular on six, please." He tried his best to be polite.

"Three on six," the clerk repeated. He looked up briefly and saw the beautiful red Caddy parked in front of pump six, and the incongruity of the order amused him. He might have tried to suppress a smirk, but it showed nevertheless.

"Three big ones on. . . " he began, but didn't finish the sentence.

Teddy had reached over and grabbed the clerk's lapels, pulling his upper torso forward, so that they were, for a brief moment, uncomfortably intimate.

"I said three dollars, motherfucker," Teddy whispered to the clerk, who was now silent and afraid. "Your black ass *comprende?*"

He nodded and Teddy released him. "Good," he said, as he turned to leave. "Keep the change, chump."

Teddy quickly pumped the gas—three dollars doesn't buy much—then waved the nozzle and left it on the ground. Next, he slowly got behind the steering wheel. As he turned his car into traffic, the episode was quickly forgotten; his mind was on other things. Sugar was nestled close, rubbing her hand inside his shirt and over his belly and chest.

"Baby," he said suddenly after an uncharacteristic silence. "I think we gotta stop by the rectory."

Sugar was disappointed. "But you said. . . " she began.

Teddy cut her short; his tone was pleasant but firm. "It's serious," he said solemnly. "I got feelin's."

Ben would have understood, but Sugar was puzzled. She could tell, though, that her man had made up his mind. Further argument would be useless.

It was a funny thing about Teddy. Even as a boy, he always had "feelin's," though he took great pains to deny any trace of a religious or spiritual connection. They didn't come often, just enough, and sometimes at opportune moments, like when his hamster was hopelessly lost in the house. Ben and he had spent three futile days searching. Then, while they were seated in the kitchen, morosely sipping Cokes, Teddy suddenly stood up. "Let's go," he said excitedly. "I see him."

He was there, too, a bit thinner but otherwise OK. The hamster was standing on his hind legs at the foot of the basement stairway, and Teddy went straight to the spot.

There were other times as well, far more meaningful, like his year in Vietnam, when his survival on two occasions could only be explained by his gift.

When he was young, it used to bother him. "What if," he once confessed to Ben, "I see you or mom or me go? Then what?" Ben had no answer. But as time progressed, Teddy became consumed with other matters, against which his feelin's competed unsuccessfully.

By adulthood, they appeared only occasionally, like those two times in Vietnam, and once after he had been mustered out in California. It was there he first took to burglarizing homes. On one night, the owner was hidden behind a divan, showing only his eyes, hands, and the black barrel of a six-inch .38-caliber.

As Teddy sorted through the family silver, he suddenly knew something was wrong. He also knew that any quick movement would mean his end. Even screwed up as he was then, Teddy wasn't quite ready for that.

"You got me," he said loudly, and he slowly raised his hands away from his body. Given the owner's fear and anxiety, Teddy's feelin's saved him then, too, though not from prison. It was his second arrest, and conviction was guaranteed—with no probation.

In the joint, he had time to think, and one of the things he constantly thought about was his gift. Eventually, he concluded it worked best only in regard to those he cared for. Even then, the list was short and, after his mom died, that meant mostly him. After he was released and returned to Seattle, he added Ben. He was even starting to think that, at some point, Sugar might join them.

Teddy pushed the gas pedal to the floor, and within a few minutes, he could see the distinctive single spire of St. Mary's. There used to be two, but one fell off in a windstorm, so the strapped parishioners voted then to top it. That was twenty years ago.

He stopped a half block from the rectory, unsure of what it was he felt. A robbery or a burglary, maybe worse. He didn't know and couldn't tell. All he knew was that something was buzzing, loud and constant in the back of his head, that hadn't been there since California or Vietnam.

Teddy pulled his gun and turned toward Sugar. "Somethin's cookin', Baby. Gotta check it out. You stay here, OK?"

"I'm goin', Teddy," she said firmly. It was clear her mind was made up. He didn't argue; there wasn't enough time.

"All right," he said. "Just take off them high-heel sneakers." He pointed to her black high heels with open toes and backs. "Save 'em for bed," he added with a smile before moving quickly out of the car.

Sugar joined him, and together they approached the rectory, crouched like assassins, avoiding what little light there was. They checked the rear and sides; there was no sign of forced entry. The building was dark, except for a small light in Ben's room. They walked to the front. The door was locked. Teddy rang the bell. No answer. He then tried the door knob. It was also locked. Teddy opened the door with his key, taking care to stand to the side as he turned the handle and pushed. He snuck one, then two peeks inside the dark hallway before reaching inside for the light switch. He peeked once more, then entered, motioning for Sugar to follow.

"Angelo," he called. There was still no answer. The light came from Ben's room at the top of the stairway in the hall. He told Sugar to wait. Quickly and quietly, he ascended the stairs alone, positioning himself, as before, to one side of Ben's door.

"Angelo," he said again, and again there was no answer. The door was slightly ajar, and Teddy gulped a deep breath to calm himself. His head throbbed with a sharp tympanic rhythm, loud and distracting, like a metronome in an otherwise silent room. He had felt it before, and he expected the worst as he pushed the door open.

Gun and eyes first, he told himself, body second.

He squared up, both hands on the semi-automatic, ready to fire. For a brief and frightening moment, he was pointing the gun at Ben, who was seated at his desk, his back toward Teddy.

Teddy quickly scanned the room. Everything was in order, or seemed that way but something, Teddy felt, was terribly wrong.

"Angelo," he said softly as he holstered his gun and approached his friend. He stopped, frozen in place by Ben's words and tone of voice.

"I'm a dead man," Ben said without turning. His voice was even, distant, and coldly rational—like a tape of the weather report.

"What?"

"But no guts," he continued. "At least not yet. It's all just a matter of time, though. Just a matter of time."

Teddy sensed Ben's desperate need for distance and, rather than approach him directly, walked off to the side toward the bed. He sat on the edge. His friend seemed not to notice and continued to stare straight ahead.

"I looked for your gun," Ben said calmly, "but I forgot you take it with you to Sugar's." He chuckled. "I thought about a knife, but it's too painful. You know, if you go across the wrist you might miss the artery."

Ben then pointed to a nearly empty bottle of sleeping pills. "And these," he said disgustedly. "There weren't enough of these. Popped a couple, though. Just enough to get sick on."

Teddy was stunned. Ben was discussing different ways of suicide like others shop Fords and Chevys.

"At least I should go back," Ben added calmly. "I have an obligation. Maybe she had family; maybe I can help. Maybe I can. . . "

Teddy interrupted him. "Man, what're you talkin' about? Don't talk trash. Stop talkin' like that." He was trying to sound authoritative and confident without pushing too much, but he could feel a creeping sense of panic and hopelessness.

". . . beg forgiveness," Ben said finally without looking at his friend. Before speaking again, he turned slowly toward Teddy, making sure that their eyes locked. "Teddy," he asked softly, "you know how she died?"

"Who?"

"Ellen," he said. The question surprised Teddy, rendering him speechless. He thought the matter had long been laid to rest.

"Abortion," Ben whispered, his eyes dark with shock and grief. "Clara just told me. My kid, I guess."

For Teddy, the last few days were some of the most difficult he could recall. The lost days in California—including two years in prison—and the year in Vietnam, those times were hard, but of a different sort. He was younger then, full of himself and confident that there was, somewhere, a long, hidden tunnel stocked with tomorrows. Besides, he was living then just for himself, no one else, and part of that meant choices with prices he was willing to pay.

The moral implications of Vietnam destroyed some of his buddies, but not Teddy. He was immune because he didn't think in moral terms. He found he liked combat, the noise and confusion, but what he liked best was the excitement of survival. Shooting and killing, or being shot and being killed, were aspects and costs incidental to the adventure.

In California, he found that he missed it all, particularly the surge of adrenalin that he had come to expect and enjoy. Burglary was his substitute. To a degree, the thrill returned for a while, and then it was over.

Prison changed him, that and the coming of age. Inside he saw too many men, isolated and alone, their lives and deaths meaningless even to themselves. He knew then he wanted more. When Teddy returned to Seattle, he realized that Ben was still Angelo, his friend forever, and the main link between his old life and something better.

And now, Teddy thought, the motherfucker's checkin' out.

He aimed to prevent it. That week, Teddy stayed close to Ben, watching for signs, listening for feelin's. Outwardly Ben seemed fine, and assured Teddy that such was the case. For his part, Teddy was careful not to push; he knew Ben's way and understood the heavy burden he now carried. This time, he didn't have a "Zorro" story.

For Catholics, which Teddy still nominally was, abortion was a mortal sin; and Ellen's death doubled its gravity. Teddy also knew that on some high, esoteric plane, Ben was free of guilt—he didn't order the abortion or in any way encourage it. But he'd never seen those heights, and suspected only angels had, not humans with blood in their veins. The deaths of Ellen and her unborn child had touched Ben like a brush, staining him with guilt he knew time wouldn't erase. He hoped it might heal. Even then, he wasn't sure.

Teddy was leery, thinking Ben's improvement might be a pose, but slowly he began to change his mind. "Relax," Ben said. "I wasn't my normal self. I've had a chance to think since then, and it's under control. Suicide's no answer; neither's going back. I understand now that it wasn't my fault."

Teddy looked at his friend, not certain what to believe.

"Look," Ben added. "I figure that people have choices, and Ellen made hers. I didn't force her. I couldn't know... " Ben paused before speaking. He knew Teddy needed more proof. "Go to my room, man," he said reassuringly. "Check it out; got no ticket for Manila."

Teddy stared at his friend; his speech was persuasive. By Friday Teddy was confident enough to go out with Sugar, but before leaving, he took some precautions. He hid the sharp kitchen knives, emptied the medicine cabinet, and took Ben's keys to "Janis." He also returned after two hours to check on his friend and found him alone in his room.

It seemed innocent enough. Ben was lying on his bed, reading a newspaper and sipping a beer. Everything seemed fine.

Ben scolded his friend as he entered the room. "I told you I'm OK," he said. Upon hearing that, Teddy turned abruptly and walked back out, his feelin's nowhere to be found. As he closed the rectory door he ran straight to the car, feeling lighter and quicker than he had in days. His destination was Sugar's. He hoped she was where he left her, in bed. If he hurried, his spot would still be warm.

It was early Saturday afternoon, a half hour before confessions. Ben was kneeling by his bed, his face buried in his hands, seeking comfort in the darkness there. He was praying for forgiveness he didn't think would come. For how long, he wasn't sure, but it must have been hours. His body was soaked in sweat, like he had just sat in a sauna, and his knees felt raw and his back was sore.

Almost by accident, he glanced at the clock and started to rise slowly to his feet. His problem would have to wait, it was time for those of others. If he hurried, he thought he could grab a quick shower and a cup of instant coffee.

People depended on him, particularly those seeking absolution. Ben was a good priest, his stay in Manila aside. Despite his troubles, he would try not to let anyone down.

The first hour in the confessional passed quickly. The weekly regulars were there, including the lonely old black woman and the guilt-ridden adolescent, plus a few others who came less regularly than the first two. The sins confessed were nothing extraordinary—outbursts of anger and impatience, impurity of thought, and even one case of illicit sex (a young college student confessed to sex with a prostitute at his best friend's recent bachelor party).

Ben called it a "laundry list" of sins, minimal transgressions on any scale of errors, save, perhaps, their own. Their salvations were assured. He believed his was less so, and he envied them their innocence.

He had come to love the sacrament of penance, and even its most visible sign—the oblong, upright confessional box. To him, it had become a profound symbol of human nature, in its frailty and in its consuming need to seek and receive compassion. He knew that by listening to their "sins," many of which weren't, and in dispensing God's mercy, he was touching them in a way no other human could.

It satisfied him deeply to do so; few of his other duties and sacramental powers so moved him.

As he sat there, the full gravity of Ellen's abortion and death hit him once more. He wondered who, in turn, could touch him.

For a brief, desperate moment, he thought perhaps no one— and he broke into a cold sweat. The confessional box, comfortable a few moments before, suddenly seemed stifling and ominously restrictive. Instinctively, he started to rise, reaching for the door handle. Not even the sound of a penitent entering could make him stay.

"I'll be right back," he mumbled quickly.

Outside the church, he sat on the concrete steps. He lit a cigarette, a habit since Manila, and took long, deep breaths. The cool spring air was fresh and welcome, seeming to clear his head.

He told himself he had to regain control; this wasn't his time, it belonged to others. He shook his back and head, shuddering like a retriever just from the lake. It felt good, relaxing muscles in his shoulders and neck.

He inspected the cigarette. It was almost gone, down to one more drag. He sucked deep before flinging the filter in the direction of the sidewalk. He then stood and turned toward the church's thick, hardwood doors, disappearing within a few seconds later.

Ben had been gone maybe ten minutes, but when he returned the penitent was still there. He entered the confessional and sat down, a bit embarrassed, and turned toward the black screen to offer his apology.

"I'm sorry you had to wait," he said. "There were matters I had to attend to.

"It's OK," came the quiet reply.

"Let's continue then," Ben said.

The penitent quickly began, but in a whispered voice Ben had trouble hearing. He was a young male, that much was clear, and he spoke English with a heavy Filipino accent. Ben thought immediately of the Filipino boy who tried to confess in Tagalog a few weeks ago. Maybe he's returned. If so, Ben wanted to help, not frighten or frustrate him.

He tried to put him at ease. "You're doing fine, my son, but speak just a bit louder and much slower. God loves you very much, and His forgiveness has no limit. It's his servants like me who are flawed.

"So please," he added, "once again, but slower and louder."

Ben's approach seemed to work. The young man followed his suggestion, speaking slowly and no longer in a whisper. He listed a number of sins—fighting, drunkenness, and rampant and casual sex—more serious than the usual Saturday fare.

The range and the gravity of the offenses surprised Ben. He was momentarily silent as the penitent continued.

"My son," Ben said, interrupting him, "where were you when these things were taking place."

"All over, Padre," he said.

Ben pushed the question. "Well, where?"

"Oh," he said, "parties, restaurants, bars. It don't matter, I just go with my *compadres*."

"Filipinos?"

"Ilocanos."

"When did you come here?"

"Seattle?"

"Yes," Ben answered.

"Three months ago," he said.

"From where?"

"Santa Maria, Ilocos Norte Province."

Ben paused. He knew from his mother and her friends the reputations carried by different parts of the Philippines. Filipinos born there treated such characterizations and stereotypes, broadly drawn though they were, as articles of faith, more reasons to distinguish and divide a hopelessly divided people.

Ben was vaguely aware that the Ilocos region was less fertile than the others, and its harsh, unyielding land produced hardy, quick-tempered, and fearless folk. He also knew that in Seattle and other West Coast cities, there were large Ilocano communities, many of their members in their seventies who came to this country a half century earlier. Their migration said much about the hardship of life back home and more about the sense of adventure possessed by young men willing to leave family, friends, and everything familiar.

Beyond that, Ben paid little attention to the regional differences dear to immigrant hearts. He figured that his home was the U.S., not some barrio of Cebu.

"Ilocano, eh?" Ben continued.

"Yes sir," the young man said proudly. "I mean, Padre," he added politely, correcting himself.

"How old are you son?" Ben's tone was warm and concerned.

"Nineteen, Padre," he said.

"How old are your friends?"

"Twenties," he said, "maybe thirties. I'm not sure."

For Ben, the picture was quickly coming together. His older companions were obviously a fast, street-wise group, a powerful and bad influence on a naive, recently arrived immigrant. He'd seen them before and knew their kind; the link would have to be severed.

"Son," Ben said, "I think... "

"Padre," the young man said, interrupting him, "I have something else to say." His voice was dropping, nearing a whisper.

"Padre," he said again.

"Yes, my son."

"I killed someone."

Ben was stunned. In all of his years as a priest, he had never heard those words spoken. Not even Arsenio on his deathbed said that; he admitted only to being there while others did the work.

Ben could feel himself tense, and he knew that his heart was racing. He waited a moment, using the time to calm himself.

"That's a very serious offense," he said. Ben was trying hard to make sure his inflection was, or seemed, natural. He hoped it worked. "Did you kill in self-defense?"

"Yes."

"Can you explain?"

"This guy gives my *compadre* hard looks. So my *compadre* says to us, 'Gotta kick his ass.' So we do."

For Ben, the penitent's story was uncomfortably familiar. He knew it was the altercation in Chinatown which had claimed Artie's life, setting in motion the as-yet-unfinished cycle of violence. His sense of fear was now balanced by an infusion of anger and revulsion, and, for a moment, he thought of just walking out of the confessional. He calmed himself, though, by recalling that his duty was not to himself but to others. The young man sought absolution, and if his sorrow was genuine, it was his duty to grant it.

Ben didn't press for more specifics on the killing. It wasn't necessary and, more important, he didn't want to know.

"That isn't self-defense, son," Ben said evenly. "What you did was murder."

There was silence for a moment before the penitent replied. "Oh," he said.

"It's a very serious sin, a mortal sin," Ben continued gravely, "and God needs for you to be truly sorry before absolution can be granted."

"Padre," the young man cried, "I want to be forgiven."

Ben could hear him sobbing quietly. His breath was short and his sense of desperation evident.

"I might die, Father," he said. "I don't know, but I might die."

Payback, Ben thought, cycle-completing, and Teddy's warning to stay out of the way.

"Now, calm down," Ben said firmly. "You're safe here." Ben wondered if *he* was safe here.

"Just listen, please," Ben said. "Absolution depends upon genuine sorrow. In your case, genuine sorrow also depends on your giving up friends, companions, and situations that could lead to sin. Are you willing to do this?"

There was no response.

"Will you do this?" Ben repeated.

"No," he said.

Ben didn't expect that answer. "But don't you see I can't absolve you of a mortal sin unless... "

"Padre," the young man interrupted, "I cannot give up my *barkada*."

Barkada. That word again. All for one, one for all, and us against the world.

"Look," Ben said firmly, "your *barkada* leads you to sin, serious sin, and if your sorrow is genuine, you must be willing to give it up."

"Padre," the penitent cried, "I can't."

"Then," Ben replied, "I cannot grant you absolution."

The young man was crying now. "Padre," he said between sobs, "I came to you because I heard you're Filipino and you'd understand. You're hurting my feelings, Padre. You don't understand."

"I understand," Ben said.

"No, you don't," he argued, "not like a real Filipino. Back home, there'd be no problem."

Ben was trying hard not to become angry. "You're not back home now," he said. "Things are different here."

"Please, Padre?" The voice was desperate, and Ben sensed the young man might be losing it.

"No," he said firmly with more than a hint of anger. "I think we should conclude this."

"*Demonyo!*" the young man spat.

Ben knew he had been cursed, and he was glad the ordeal was over. He could hear the young Filipino stand up and open the door. Ben felt his warm face, and wiped the perspiration off with his sleeve. He looked at his watch; a few more minutes and he was free to leave.

Ben took a deep breath and tried to relax. As he started to exhale, the door suddenly swung open. Standing there was the young Filipino penitent. Ben knew it was he. In his hand was a small caliber revolver, its short barrel pointed at Ben's chest.

"Son a bitch," he spat. "I want absolution."

His eyes were glazed and unfocused. It was obvious to Ben that the boy had lost it, temporarily or permanently he wasn't sure—Jesus! Do I save myself? Do I comply?—Ben felt his belly tighten, his heartbeat rise, his mouth go dry.

"I said I want it," the boy repeated.

"Put the gun down, son," Ben said, trying to be calm.

"One more time, Padre." The boy's trigger hand shook as he spoke. The gun could go off accidentally.

Ben made up his mind. He'd try to talk him out of it, but under no condition would absolution be granted, or even feigned. Choices, he thought. For Ben, the sacrament was precious, absolute, not to be profaned. Besides, ironically, death might very well mean absolution for a priest.

Or maybe not. Paradox. Given his own longing for absolution, would such a death... would it be suicide, barring the gate to Christian burial but opening the one to hell?

Afraid, he hesitated for just a second, but gathered himself before speaking. Shit, he thought, let God decide.

"No," Ben said firmly.

A drunken sleep punctuated by an ominous vision. Teddy and Sugar had stayed out all Friday night, supplementing their usual fare of a movie and a bite to eat with drinking and dancing at an after-hours club. Friday was Teddy's payday, so there was money to spend. Plus, he was relieved that Ben seemed finally to have recovered. The preceding days had been tense, and he intended to relax.

The revelers returned to Sugar's at four in the morning, too tired and drunk to make it to her bedroom, much less disrobe and make love. Teddy flopped face first onto the large living room couch, and Sugar, vaguely aware of her man's location, attempted to join him. She didn't quite make it though, bouncing off his back and onto the carpeted floor.

That's how they stayed until Saturday afternoon, when Teddy sat straight up, lifting like a rocket from its pad. The pain followed immediately.

"Shit," he said as he felt first his head, which throbbed at different points, then his thighs and lower back, where the aches were less percussive but more uniform. The combination forced him back down.

He looked at his watch, then at his gun, which had fallen to the floor during the night, and, finally, at Sugar, who was five feet away. "Shit," he said again.

He had intended to return to the rectory at about noon, but it was long past that. He reached for a cigarette, lit it, and tried to recall something he knew was important. It was hard; his head hurt and his mind was fogged.

He forced himself to sit up, this time more slowly, and

closed his eyes. Concentrate, he told himself, concentrate. Slowly, his mind started to clear. He had had a dream, a nightmare, the latter a rare occurrence since there was little that frightened or disturbed him. He had seen snips of pictures from a place far away. Maybe Vietnam? he thought. Not likely, he concluded. He had enjoyed his tour, and war had produced no nightmares for him. But the terrain, the vegetation, and the people were similar.

The dream now started to return, in larger pictures, as his mind continued to clear. Effortlessly, he spanned mountains and valleys like a camera from a jet. Narrow focus now, to a wooded hilltop and a ledge with a blood-red surface. On that ledge was a cross, crudely made, from which hung the body of a man.

He shuddered. Strange stuff, a dream with religious overtones. Easter was long over and Christmas was still months away. It had been years since he had had one of those and it bothered him. Why, exactly he couldn't tell. He kept his eyes closed, trying harder to focus. No luck. Whatever was there was now gone, with only the traces he held remaining.

He dragged the cigarette hard, one suck left. As he did, he felt a sharp pain, deep in his chest, tit level right side. It was sharper than the others and, reflexively, his body tilted toward it.

Gotta cut down, he thought disgustedly as he placed the filter in an ashtray, and soon.

On days when it doesn't rain, June in Manila is drab and hot. The rich survive by keeping their air conditioning on twenty-four hours a day, or by visiting beach homes by the sea. The poor just survive.

But even for the rich, there are prices that sometimes cannot be paid, like brownouts when the city's generators fail from overuse. The air-cons are silent in the luxury hotels, and even the wealthy make do as best they can.

For Clara Natividad, making do meant flying down to Cebu City in her private plane, to her auxiliary office in the house on Mango Street. Her pilot had just completed take-off, and Clara leaned back in the seat, eyes closed, composing her mind before she turned to a review of business papers.

As she often did of late, she thought of Remedios's death in March and of her boy Ben and his all-too-brief journey to the Philippines. Clara hadn't seen Ben before his abrupt departure. The business out of town—down south to her banana plantation on Mindanao—had taken much longer than she expected. There were troublesome labor organizers, and disposing of them took money and the necessary connections. No matter. She knew poor Ellen had entertained her nephew well, far better than she, and Clara smiled at the thought. Pity, though, about her and Ben.

Clara then turned to the matter at hand. There were business meetings, but they were planned for later in the afternoon. To prepare for them, she was reviewing a variety of papers, one set comprised of correspondence between herself and the Japanese owner of a large Manila hotel. She was offering to buy and he to sell, the only question being price.

As she read, with her left hand she absently patted the arm of the young woman in the seat beside her, who, childlike, had lain her head on Clara's shoulder.

"It's OK," she said softly, like she was talking to a cat or a baby. "It's OK."

"Are you sure?" her companion asked.

"It's OK," Clara repeated and continued reading.

"I hope so," the young woman said.

Some forty minutes later, the pilot was approaching the airport near Cebu City. Below them, to the south, lay the village of Talisay and, to the west, the Toledo Road meandered like a question mark through the hills.

Clara finished her review and put the papers in her brief case. She resumed petting the young woman, gently rubbing the back, then the palm of her hand across the nape of her neck.

"Are you sure?" she asked again.

"Yes," said Clara, soothingly confident. "I know him. Trust your Tia on this. I've made arrangements and he'll be here."

Clara's assurance seemed convincing. She had always come through before, and now should be no different. The young woman wiped away a tear that had started to trickle down her face.

"I hope so," Ellen said.